SUFISM FOR NON-SUFIS?

SUFISM FOR NON-SUFIS?

Ibn 'Aṭā' Allāh al-Sakandarī's Tāj al-'Arūs

Sherman A. Jackson

OXFORD
UNIVERSITY PRESS

OXFORD
UNIVERSITY PRESS

Oxford University Press, Inc., publishes works that further
Oxford University's objective of excellence
in research, scholarship, and education.

Oxford New York
Auckland Cape Town Dar es Salaam Hong Kong Karachi
Kuala Lumpur Madrid Melbourne Mexico City Nairobi
New Delhi Shanghai Taipei Toronto

With offices in
Argentina Austria Brazil Chile Czech Republic France Greece
Guatemala Hungary Italy Japan Poland Portugal Singapore
South Korea Switzerland Thailand Turkey Ukraine Vietnam

Published by Oxford University Press, Inc.
198 Madison Avenue, New York, New York 10016

www.oup.com

Library of Congress Cataloging-in-Publication Data
Ibn 'Ata' Allah, Ahmad ibn Muhammad, d. 1309.
[Tāj al-'arūs al-ḥāwī li-tahdhīb al-nufus. English]
Sufism for non-sufis? : Ibn 'Aṭā' Allāh al-Sakandarī's Tāj al-'arūs / [translated by] Sherman A. Jackson.
p. cm.
Translated from Arabic.
Includes index.
ISBN 978-0-19-987367-8 (hardcover : alk. paper)
1. Sufism—Early works to 1800. 2. Religious life—Islam—Early works to 1800. I. Jackson,
Sherman A. II. Title. III. Title: Ibn 'Aṭā' Allāh al-Sakandarī's Tāj al-'arūs.
BP188.9.I25713 2012
297.4—dc23 2011032655

To Heather

Here, my dear; here it is.

CONTENTS

ACKNOWLEDGMENTS

I would like to express my heart-felt debt to all of my students, formal and informal, whose indulgence over the years in reading, discussing and exploring the depths of this text inspired the present effort. I include here those who have attended my sessions at the Reviving the Islamic Spirit Retreat in Toronto Canada. And I am especially grateful to those who filled my classes at the American Learning Institute for Muslims (*ALIM*) in Michigan. It is they, in fact, who first alerted me to the value a work like this could have for young people, who, contrary to the expectations of many, remain sensitive and attracted to a life of spiritual refinement. I hope that they will not only recognize herein the spirit of our many exchanges but that they will be inspired by what they detect to be my own evolution in understanding and appreciating Ibn 'Aṭā' Allāh. I would also like to thank Professor Alexander Knysh of the University of Michigan for kindly reading and commenting on an early version of the Introduction. A very special thanks goes to OUP editor Cynthia Read, whose sustained confidence in this project nursed it through several 'salutary iterations'. In this same context, I would like to thank OUP's anonymous reviewers, whose integrity and perspicacious judgment spared me embarrassment that I would otherwise prefer not to think about. I would also like to express my appreciation to my children, Hassan, Shihab, Saphia and Niyyah, for their undying support and for putting up with me, the distracted dad, throughout this project. Over the years, I have held off on dedicating any of my books to my wife, because I did not want this to be an empty, pro-forma exercise. I wanted it to attach to something in which I felt she could take a genuine interest and from which she might derive genuine benefit. I hope I have found this in Ibn ʿAṭāʾ Allāh's *Tāj al-ʿArūs*. And it is on this hope that I dedicate this humble effort to my wife, Heather R. Laird.

SUFISM FOR NON-SUFIS?

Introduction

> The mastery of nature is vainly
> believed to be an adequate substitute for self-mastery.
>
> —Reinhold Niebuhr

Tāj al-ʿArūs al-Ḥāwī li Tahdhīb al-Nufūs, a full translation of which I present here under the title, *The Bride-Groom's Crown Containing Instructions on Refining the Self,* is, as its title suggests, a work on spiritual[1] education. Its author, Ibn ʿAṭāʾ Allāh al-Sakandarī, was a celebrated Sufi in the premodern tradition of Islam. Given the modern polemic around Sufism,[2] this alone might be enough to discourage many, especially non-Sufis, from taking any interest in such

1. Throughout this introduction, my use of the term "spiritual" pays homage to modern convention and recognizes—perhaps more than it should—the modern dichotomy posited between "spirituality" and "materialism." On this dichotomy, at least from the perspective of those who support the former against the latter, spirituality is deemed to be categorically and incontrovertibly positive. By contrast, part of Islam's essential struggle from the very beginning was to identify good, substantively sound spirituality and distinguish it from and elevate it over bad, misguided spirituality. In sum, not all spirituality was or is good. It may be some time, however, before the language of modern religious discourse can recover to the point that it enables us to express this idea in terms that are concise, clear, and simple enough to make it worth the while.
2. See, e.g., V. J. Cornell, "Practical Sufism: An Akbarian Basis for a Liberal Theology of Difference," *Islamic Law and Culture,* vol. 9 no. 2 (Winter 2004): 103–126, especially 104–109, where he surveys the major "criticisms leveled at the Sufi tradition by its modern Muslim opponents."

a text. But *The Bride-Groom's Crown* so quickly defies many of the criticisms and stereotypes popularized by Sufism's modern opponents that it soon reveals many of these popular misgivings to be misplaced. At the same time, it challenges modern proponents of Sufism, by intimating alternatives to mysticism (particularly where it entails or implies pantheism) as the pivotal focus of the Sufi enterprise. To be sure, Ibn 'Aṭā' Allāh was an active participant in the pre-modern debate around Sufism. In this text, however, he largely steps away from this concern and devotes himself more directly to ingratiating the common Muslim with Sufism's *sine qua non,* that is, a direct, deep-seated, and proper relationship with God, above and beyond all other spiritual concerns or "achievements." In this capacity, *The Bride-Groom's Crown* represents a minimalist approach to Sufism, its minimalism functioning not as an ideal but as a means of reaching and inspiring everyday believers and elevating their moral, spiritual, and devotional confidence and resolve.

To be sure, the "everyday believers" of Ibn 'Aṭā' Allāh's time are separated from their contemporary coreligionists by the historical *cum*-civilizational boundary of modernity. As such, Ibn 'Aṭā' Allāh obviously could not craft his message to speak to them directly. Like all great works, *The Bride-Groom's Crown* includes a transcendent element capable of standing on its own and speaking to us all as simply humans. But to speak to modern Muslims in the very specific and concrete context of the events, contests, and adjustments that have come to define their lives requires an act of "translation." This is the aim of this introduction, even as I recognize that Ibn 'Aṭā' Allāh's text might also be read against a backdrop of experiences and or understandings that differ from or perhaps even contradict what I have taken to be among *the* seminal features of modernity for Muslims.[3]

3. See the section, "Modern Relevance," below.

I. IBN 'AṬĀ' ALLĀH

Tāj al-Dīn Abū al-Faḍl (also Abū al-'Abbās) Aḥmad b. Muḥammad b. 'Abd al-Karīm b. 'Abd al-Raḥmān b. 'Abd Allāh b. Aḥmad b. 'Īsā b. al-Ḥusayn Ibn 'Aṭā' Allāh al-Iskandarī or al-Sakandarī was born in Alexandria, Egypt, and later moved to Cairo, where he died in 709/1309. He was a Mālikī in law[4] and an Ash'arite in theology.[5] He was a pupil of the famous Sufi master, Abū al-'Abbās al-Mursī (d. 686/1287), who was actually of Spanish origin and the leading protégé of the even more famous eponym of the Sufi order to which they all belonged, Abū al-Ḥasan al-Shādhilī (d. 656/1258). Al-Shādhilī was born in Morocco around 583/1187 and reared in the Sufi tradition there, though he also traveled to and studied in the East.[6] On instructions from his master, 'Abd al-Salām Ibn Mashīsh (d. 625/1228), he moved to a place called Shādhilah in Tunisia, from which he took the name "al-Shādhilī." He later moved to Alexandria, Egypt in 642/1244 or 650/1252, accompanied by Abū al-'Abbās al-Mursī. It was here that Ibn 'Aṭā' Allāh would come under his tutelage.

In North Africa, early Sufism had come under attack for some of its doctrinal and practical excesses and unsanctioned innovations, particularly by the upholders of Mālikī orthodoxy, men no less in stature than Yaḥyā b. 'Umar (d. 289/901) and Ibn Abī Zayd al-Qayrawānī (d. 386/996). In fact, later Mālikī jurists would go so

4. This is explicitly affirmed by Aḥmad Zarrūq in the introduction to his commentary on Ibn 'Aṭā' Allāh's *Ḥikam*. See *Ḥikam ibn 'aṭā' Allāh: sharḥ al-'ārif bi Allāh al-shaykh zarrūq*, ed. 'A. Maḥmūd and M. Ibn al-Sharīf (Cairo: al-Sha'b, N.d.), 37.
5. This may explain why the Shāfi'ī-Ash'arite propagandist Tāj al-Dīn al-Subkī claims him as a Shāfi'ī.
6. In the introduction to *Laṭā'if al-minan*, Sh. 'Abd al-Ḥalīm Maḥmūd notes that al-Shādhilī used to teach from al-Ghazālī's *Iḥyā 'ulūm al-dīn*, Abū Ṭālib al-Makkī's *Qūt al-qulūb* and al-Qushayrī's *al-Risālah al-qushayrīya*, all of which we might assume him to have studied while in the East. See Ibn 'Aṭā' Allāh, *Laṭā'if al-minan*, ed. 'Abd al-Ḥalīm Maḥmūd 2nd ed. (Cairo: Dār al-Ma'ārif, N.d.), 11.

far as to prevail upon the Almoravid ruler, Yūsuf Ibn Tashufīn (r. 453–500/1061–1106), to conduct a public burning of al-Ghazālī-'s famous *Iḥyā' 'Ulūm al-Dīn* (*The Revivification of the Truly Religious Sciences*), which included a disquieting, "spiritualized" critique of the religious establishment and status quo. This did not occur, of course, without objections from Sufis themselves, and over time a new *modus vivendi* would emerge. By the middle of the sixth/twelfth century, Sufism would boast prominent representation in the Maghrib, while, "the dominant Malikite norms of Islamic piety in this region ensured that the patently unorthodox Sufi tenets did not gain ground in it."[7]

Al-Shādhilī's Sufism has thus been described as "moderate."[8] Indeed, he "emphasized the practical aspects of mysticism over against the more metaphysically oriented mysticism of Ibn 'Arabī and his followers."[9] He was attentive to the material life of his students, had no appetite for antinomianism, and eschewed such practices as using music to induce trances or spawn spectacular feats, such as walking on fire or piercing the flesh. Al-Shādhilī even disapproved of begging or implying the necessity of wearing special clothing that marked one a mendicant. Indeed, he himself was known to dress quite elegantly.[10] On the matter of spiritual epiphanies or mystical unveilings, he is reported to have said:

7. Jamil Abun-Nasr, *Muslim Communities of Grace: The Sufi Brotherhoods in Islamic Religious Life* (New York: Columbia University Press, 2007), 98.
8. See "al-Shādhilī, Abū al-Ḥasan," *E.I.*, 9: 170. See also A. Knysh, *Islamic Mysticism: A Short History* (Leiden: E. J. Brill, 2000), 217, where it is noted, inter alia, that, "the Shādhilī brotherhood are characterized by their strong attachment to Sunnī orthodoxy and strict observance of the letter of the Sharia. Its adherents tended to play down the importance of saintly miracles, preaching instead self-restraint and sobriety in word and deed."
9. Knysh, *Islamic Mysticism*, 210.
10. In fact, Ibn 'Aṭā' Allāh reports: "A mendicant once entered upon Shaykh Abū al-Ḥasan wearing a fur garment. When the Shaykh finished his lesson, the man approached him, reached out and sampled his clothing and said, 'O master, God is not worshipped in

> If your unveiling (*kashf*) contradicts the Qur'ān and Sunna, hold fast to the Qur'ān and Sunna and ignore your unveiling. Tell yourself, "God The Exalted has guaranteed for me the truth of The Book and The Sunna, which He did not do in the case of unveiling, inspiration (*ilhām*) and direct witnessing (*mushāhadah*)," not to mention the fact that the scholars agree that it is not permissible to act on the basis of unveiling, inspiration or direct witnessing, without first comparing these with The Book and The Sunna.[11]

Al-Shādhilī left no systematic writings; nor did his immediate successor and eventual son-in-law, Abū al-'Abbās al-Mursī. The task of developing Shādhilī doctrine fell thus to Ibn 'Aṭā' Allāh, who succeeded al-Mursī as head of the order. Ibn 'Aṭā' Allāh clearly continued with the teachings of his masters but also appears to have been influenced by mystical doctrines from the East, not to mention, most probably, those of the controversial Muḥyī al-Dīn Ibn 'Arabī.[12] This may explain, in part at least, his standing, bitter disagreement

---

clothing like the ones you are wearing.' The Shaykh reached out and sampled the man's clothing and, noticing how course they were, said, 'God is not worshipped in clothing like the ones *you* are wearing. My clothing say that I am not in need of the people, so they do not have to give me anything. Your clothing say that you are in need of the people, so they should give you something.'" Ibn 'Aṭā' Allāh adds that the point of this is not to condemn those who wear clothing that mark them as Sufis but to affirm that no special clothing is required. Indeed, he says, "There is no blame on those who wear such clothing nor on those who do not, assuming that they are among those who practice righteousness." See *Laṭā'if al-minan,* 161.

11. See 'Abd al-Wahhāb b. Aḥmad. b. 'Alī al-Sha'rānī, *al-Ṭabaqāt al-kubrā* (a.k.a. *Lawāqiḥ al-anwār fī ṭabaqāt al-akhyār*), ed. 'A.M.'A. al-Fāsī (Beirut: Dār al-Kutub al-'Ilmīyah, 2006), 291.

12. Abun-Nasr, *Communities,* 107. See also Knysh, *Islamic Mysticism,* 217, where it is noted that Shādhilīs were known to embrace and write commentaries on Ibn 'Arabī's teachings, as part of a strategy of reaching out to different layers of Muslims, especially "high brows." Meanwhile, in the introduction to *Kitāb hatk al-astār fī 'ilm al-asrār,* ed. M.'A. al-Shāghūlī (al-Maktabah al-Azharīyah li al-Turāth, N.d.), 13, the editor states explicitly that Ibn 'Aṭā'

with Ibn Taymīya.[13] And yet, despite their differences, both men effectively agreed that exaggerations existed on both sides of the Sufi divide.[14] On the one hand, Ibn 'Aṭā' Allāh warns against those, "especially scholars," who impugn the very efficacy of the Sufi enterprise. [¶256] At the same time, he sharply criticizes those Sufi charlatans whose treachery and depravity end up turning people away from the spiritual path. [¶270][15]

Ibn 'Aṭā' Allāh is reported to have authored some twenty works, in fields ranging from Sufism to Qur'ānic exegesis to hadith, grammar, and legal methodology.[16] Of these, his *Laṭā'if al-Minan* (*Subtle Divine Graces*),[17] which included hagiographical biographies of his two masters, al-Shādhilī and al-Mursī, is said to have represented "the principal statement of the Shādhilī teaching."[18] By far, however, the most popular and influential of his works was *al-Ḥikam al-'Aṭā'īyah* (*Wise 'Aṭā'īyan Sayings*),[19] a tightly constructed, riveting trove of Sufi aphorisms. A third, widely known treatise, also on Sufism, was his *Kitāb al-Tanwīr fī Isqāṭ al-Tadbīr* (*Enlightenment on the Futility of Planning*).[20] Interestingly, *The Bride-Groom's*

Allāh relied on the works of Ibn 'Arabī in composing this text. We should note, however, that this work is a "popular" edition of a single manuscript held at the Egyptian National Library. No such title (or similar title) appears in the lists of Ibn 'Aṭā' Allāh's works provided by Brockelmann. See *Geschichte*, II: 143–144; S II: 145–147.

13. See G. Makdisi, "Ibn 'Aṭā' Allāh," *The Encyclopedia of Islam, New Edition*, 3: 722–723.
14. On Ibn Taymīya's recognition in this regard, see below, p. 23.
15. See also, below, p. 23, where Ibn Taymīya gives a similar depiction of the extremism on both sides of the Sufi divide.
16. G. Makdisi, "Ibn 'Aṭā' Allāh," *E.I.*: 3: 722.
17. Transl., N. Roberts, under the title *The Subtle Blessings in the Saintly Lives of Abu al-Abbas al-Mursi and His Master Abu al-Hasan* (Louisville, KY: Fons Vitae, 2005).
18. A. Knysh, *Islamic Mysticism*, 213.
19. Transl. V. Danner, under the title, *Ibn 'Ata' Illah: The Book of Wisdom* (New York: Paulist Press, 1978).
20. Cairo: Maṭbū'āt wa Maktabat wa Maṭba'at 'Abbās 'Abd al-Salām Shaqrūn, N.d. This work (though not necessarily this edition) has been translated by S. Kugle under the title, *The Book of Illumination* (Louisville, KY: Fons Vitae, 2005).

Crown does not come in for much mention or praise by premodern historians or biographers. This raises questions about just how representative it was of Ibn ʿAṭāʾ Allāh's thought as a fully constituted system.[21] On the other hand, it may simply reflect the fact that historians and biographers were little interested in the particular *genre* of Sufi writing represented by *The Bride-Groom's Crown*: a substantively rich and serious yet palpably popular articulation of Sufism's *raison d'ētre*.

II. SUFISM FOR NON-SUFIS?

The Bride-Groom's Crown shares whole swatches of material with both *Wise ʿAṭāʾīyan Sayings* and *Enlightenment on the Futility of Planning*. Yet, the different ways and contexts in which this material is deployed suggest a plainly different set of audiences. Similarly, the extreme terseness and often cryptic locution of *Wise ʿAṭāʾīyan Sayings* immediately sets it apart from *The Bride-Groom's Crown*. While both employ an aphoristic approach, the former was clearly not meant to be consumed by "lay persons," at least not directly. This probably explains why, unlike *The Bride-Groom's Crown*, it generated numerous commentaries by some of the most venerated luminaries of the Sufi tradition. As for *Enlightenment*, it is a much more discursive text, as a result of which it is able to engage in fuller treatments of its topics. Precisely in this capacity, however, it displays a conspicuously more ideological bent, occasionally succumbing to the temptation to pepper its arguments with polemical and technical "baggage" carried over from the scholarly tradition. For example,

21. See below, p. 39, where it is established that there is no question that Ibn ʿAṭāʾ Allāh authored *The Bride-Groom's Crown*. Note also that Aḥmad Zarrūq makes explicit mention of *Tāj al-ʿarūs* in his commentary on Ibn ʿAṭāʾ Allāh's *Ḥikam*. See *Ḥikam ibn ʿaṭāʾ Allāh*, 37.

there is explicit mention and explication of the term "Sufī."[22] And there are direct and indirect jibes at Muʿtazilism (occasionally by name).[23] There are also direct and indirect allusions to formal theological topics, such as the doctrine on "objective good and evil" (*al-ḥusn wa al-qubḥ al-ʿaqlīyān*)[24] and whether God creates all human acts, obedient and disobedient (*khalq afʿāl al-ʿibād*).[25] All of this is accompanied, moreover, by a subtle yet unmistakable presence of Ashʿarite occasionalist cosmology, according to which nothing in "nature" is endowed with any efficient capacity of its own.[26]

None of this appears in *The Bride-Groom's Crown*, at least not with anything approaching this degree of explicitness or consistency. Nor is there that sense, explicitly expressed in *Enlightenment*, that not all devotees are to strive to reach the highest levels of spiritual realization. Whereas *The Bride-Groom's Crown* seems to be content with merely getting ordinary people to do their best—or perhaps just better—however far that might take them along the spiritual path, *Enlightenment* appears to be more concerned, inter alia, with overzealous adepts, warning its readers against equating *their* best with *the* best, even admonishing them against trusting themselves to go beyond a certain point.[27] According to *Enlightenment*, not everyone should try to emulate the great masters: "For those who have attained the highest spiritual states are not to be emulated (*ṣāḥib al-ḥāl lā yuqtadā bih*)."[28] By contrast, *The Bride-Groom's Crown* appears to reflect the sentiment that if a tortoise can

22. *Tanwīr*, 25.
23. *Tanwīr*, 23, 42.
24. *Tanwīr*, 24.
25. *Tanwīr*, 23.
26. See *Tanwīr*, 37, 47, 69, and passim. For more on Ash'arite occasionalist cosmology, see my *Islam and the Problem of Black Suffering* (New York: Oxford University Press, 2009), 77–78.
27. *Tanwīr*, 42, 54.
28. *Tanwīr*, 42.

simply be turned in the right direction, there is little fear of his ever outpacing himself or overshooting his desired destination.

This appeal to a broader audience is also reflected in the vocabulary, style, and overall "feel" of *The Bride-Groom's Crown*. While clearly rooted in the broader Sufi tradition,[29] it is refreshingly transparent, and with few exceptions, surprisingly sober. Mystical vignettes and allusions appear here and there, but these are clearly not the primary aim of the text and are, at any rate, unequivocally nonpantheistic. There is no mention of such constructs as *fanā'* (annihilation),[30] *baqā'* (subsistence in God), or *ḥulūl* (divine indwelling); nor do such indulgences as *tawassul* (beseeching dead saints for intercession) or *istighāthah* (beseeching dead saints for supernatural aid) receive any attention. Moreover, while Ibn 'Aṭā' Allāh clearly recognizes the positive role of mentoring, *The Bride-Groom's Crown* assumes neither the absolute necessity of a Sufi master (*shaykh/pīr*) nor his unqualified authority, let alone infallibility;[31] nor does it assume the necessity of belonging to a particular Sufi order (*ṭarīqah*) or of subscribing to a distinctly Sufi theological

29. For example, Ibn 'Aṭā' Allāh explicitly recognizes the centrality of calling the self to account (*muḥāsabah*) [¶4], which goes back to al-Ḥārith al-Muḥāsibī (d. 243/857), the notion of *jam'* (connection) [¶6], which goes back as far as al-Junayd (d. 298/910) (though perhaps not with precisely the same meaning), the controversy over whether God and humans can reciprocate intimacy [¶207], which formed the basis of the Ḥanbalite ascetic Ghulām Khalīl's (d. 275/888) accusations against Abū al-Ḥusayn al-Nūrī (d. 295/907) and the latter's subsequent trial. See Knysh, *Islamic Mysticism*, 61–62. Similarly, there is the question put to the famous al-Ḥallāj by the Ẓāhirite jurist Muḥammad b. Dā'ūd regarding the possibility of mutual love between man and God (Knysh, *Islamic Mysticism*, 74–75). Meanwhile, Ibn 'Aṭā' Allāh cites by name authorities as far back as Rābi'ah al-'Adawīyah (d. 185/801).

30. See, however, p. 80, nt. 105 below, where it is stated that one of the manuscripts does include the term "*fanā'*," though the editors apparently deem this to be a mistake.

31. Compare, e.g., the statement of Ibn 'Ajībah in his commentary on Ibn 'Aṭā' Allāh's *al-Ḥikam*, *Īqāẓ al-himam fī sharḥ al-ḥikam* (Beirut: Dār al-Kutub al-'Ilmīyah, 1417/1996), 40: "Our address is to the truly devoted disciples who are either traversing the path or who have already arrived. And we demand of them that they believe their masters (*al-ashyākh*) in everything the latter say, as they are the inheritors of the prophets."

cosmology (for example, *waḥdat al-wujūd*, "the oneness of existence"[32]); it advocates no particular régime of Sufi practice per se (for example, a formal litany or even asceticism, as a formal, institutionalized practice as opposed to an informal, recommended routine); nor is there an abundance of theologically titillating insinuations, such as those routinely conjured up by the lover-beloved trope.

In sum, *The Bride-Groom's Crown* might be read as essentially an inspirational and practical Sufi guide to self-refinement for non-Sufis. Its aim is neither to introduce new concepts, practices, or terminology; nor is it to convert or placate those who oppose Sufism in principle. Rather, its aim is simply to inspire and provide instruction on personal piety and self-refinement for those who, for historical or other reasons, have not or may never have any formal association with Sufism in any institutionalized form.

III. MODERN RELEVANCE

Ibn 'Aṭā' Allāh lived and wrote in the context of a religious, cultural, sociopolitical, and economic reality radically different from the one we now inhabit. This raises the question of the meaning and relevance of his text for modern men and women. The reality, of course, is that there is no single answer to this question, as there is no single modernity, at least not from the perspective of the actual experiences of the various peoples and civilizations across the globe. Yet, it is surely fair to assume that, to the extent that there are moderns to whom Ibn 'Aṭā' Allāh would hope to address his work, Muslims would have to top his list. And while such a focus would

32. On this doctrine, see W. C. Chittick, "*waḥdat al-wujūd*," *The Encyclopedia of Islam: New Edition*, 12 vols. (E.J. Brill, 1960–2000), 11: 37–39. See also, however, Knysh, *Islamic Mysticism*, 309–311.

clearly not exhaust the full range of *The Bride-Groom's Crown*'s semantic possibilities, exploring its meaning and utility for modern Muslims might tell us as much about the storied evolution of Islam into the modern world as it does about the premodern genius of Ibn ʿAṭāʾ Allāh.

Modernity, including Western science, secularism, consumerism, Enlightenment rationalism, modern statecraft, and their myriad accoutrements, continues to challenge theistic religion, most especially monotheism. In a sense, however, Islam's particular sociopolitical encounter with modernity sets it apart from both Judaism and Christianity. The source and nature of this divide is eloquently captured by the noted Christian theologian, John Hick, in his depiction of the early encounter between the modern West and the rest.

> [D]uring the period when it was accepted as right that Britons, Frenchmen, Germans, Dutchmen, Spaniards, Italians, and Portuguese should rule over whole black and brown populations, it was psychologically almost inevitable that they should see those whom they dominated as inferior and as in need of a higher guardianship. This categorization of black and brown humanity as inferior included their cultures and religions.[33]

33. "The Non-Absoluteness of Christianity," *The Myth of Christian Uniqueness: Toward a Pluralistic Theology of Religions*, ed., J. Hick and P. F. Knitter (Eugene, OR: Wipf and Stock, 2005), 19. Hick is hardly alone in this observation. Edward Said famously noted in *Orientalism* how the entire "orient" had been fashioned whole cloth out of the European imagination and the very negative space occupied by oriental Muslims in it. Meanwhile, J. W. Scott describes a similarly patronizing attitude on the part of the French in North Africa: "Islam was at once a symptom of Arab perversity and the cause of it, and this confusion of causality had the effect of stigmatizing both Arabs and Islam." See her *The Politics of the Veil* (Princeton, NJ: Princeton University Press, 2007), 60. Indeed, notes Scott, the great paradox of the French civilizing mission was that it was ultimately felt to be directing its energies toward a people whose inferiority actually rendered them uncivilizeable. See her *Politics*, 46–47.

Generally speaking, the challenge of how to defend religion as an institution and instill, preserve, and strengthen internally driven religiosity remains essentially the same for Islam as it is for Judaism or Christianity. Speaking more specifically, however, the fact that Islam is overwhelmingly peopled by "black and brown populations" in a world now dominated by the vision, power, and prestige of the putatively white West presents Muslims with a very distinct set of sociopolitical, cultural, and intellectual incentives and disincentives with which to negotiate the fact and expression of their religiosity. If, as Hick suggests (and one need not exaggerate his meaning here), it was "psychologically almost inevitable" for the ascendant West to designate Islam and Muslims as inferior, it should come as no surprise that Muslims might feel compelled to develop effective counters to this. Such counters, however, depending on the exigency of the moment, can end up owing more to the prerational, visceral impulse to respond to or refute perceived civilizational threats or indictments than they do to the actual teachings and sensibilities of Islam. Today, this liability typically manifests itself in either a deep-seated, often blind, protest-disposition vis-à-vis the "West," or in an equally facile attempt to negate Islam's alleged inferiority by demonstrating its unqualified compatibility with the "West."[34]

This often uncritical protest-disposition is in clear evidence among many Blackamerican Muslims, the largest single group of modern Western converts to Islam, who find in the religion, inter alia, a space from which to criticize, resist, and even opt out of the dominant order, even as they continue to appeal to God to protect and empower them in the context thereof.[35] In a similar vein, however, Muslims in and from the Muslim world routinely look to God

34. Of course, these two approaches might be united in a single individual or group.

35. On this point, see my *Islam and the Blackamerican: Looking Towards the Third Resurrection* (New York: Oxford University Press, 2005), esp., 29–57.

as divine anti-imperialist and just as often equate the mere rejection of Western ways with the establishment of a normative Islamic order. Here, moreover, the Muslim world's (read, Middle East's) putative ability to self-authenticate its articulations of Islam renders the detour around being rendered the object of another's will even more susceptible to turning into a road that leads to the total instrumentalization of Islam. This is clearly what we are witnessing in such stark and unabashed declarations as that of a modern Egyptian Islamist: "We worship God by loathing America!"[36]

Of course, one must be careful about accepting too uncritically the modern, Western redefinition-*cum*-repositioning of "religion," according to which explicitly sociopolitical or cultural contestations are placed outside the boundaries of "religion" proper.[37] On this construction, those who insist on addressing social, political, economic, or cultural issues through the prism of religion are cast in a palpably negative light, that is, as religious "fundamentalists" or as somehow "using" or "exploiting" religion for purportedly "nonreligious" ends.[38] This is especially a problem for Islam, given the Muslim tendency to

36. Tareq Hilmi, cited in R. W. Mead, *God and Gold: Britain, America and the Making of the Modern World* (New York: Alfred Knopf, 2007), 79.

37. According to some observers, this was exactly the point of this innovation. See, e.g., W. Cavanaugh, *The Myth of Religious Violence* (New York: Oxford University Press, 2009), 57–122.

38. According to Cavanaugh, the whole point of inventing the modern understanding of "religion" was to consecrate the public space as an arena where religion did not belong and to be able, thus, to deny public recognition to religious practice and judgments without this being seen as a violation of religious freedom. For, as he put it, on this new definition, "Religion is 'inward'; it is essentially about beliefs that cannot be settled publicly to the satisfaction of all by any rational method." See *Myth*, 126. Meanwhile, T. Fitzgerald goes a bit further and expresses the view that the modern invention of "religion" was/is part and parcel of a project of "cognitive imperialism serving the interests of western ideology." See his *The Ideology of Religious Studies* (New York: Oxford University Press, 2000), 13. Indeed, Fitzgerald insists, "'religion' constructs a notion of human relations divorced from power. One of the characteristics of books produced in the religion sector is that they present an idealized world of so-called faith communities—of worship, customs, beliefs, doctrines, and rites entirely divorced from the realities of power in different societies." *Ideology*, 9.

resist, seemingly more doggedly than other religious communities, the attempt to restrict "religion" to the realm of ritual and private belief. Ultimately, however, the challenge and pervasiveness of this secular perspective notwithstanding, the real question for modern Muslims is not whether protest, resistance, sustained critique, or opting out *can* be reconciled with bona fide religion on some or another good-faith interpretation. The real question is whether such postures *are* ultimately driven by preconscious, unregulated, fears, passions, and prejudices or by a principled commitment to God.

The same applies in the case of Muslims who, rather than disparage or reject the ascending order, eagerly, and often uncritically, embrace its normative status and seek to find ways to reconcile it with Islam (or vice versa). Of course, as Reinhold Niebuhr observes, power is almost always a factor in the "rational" assessments of contending groups.[39] As such, many modern Muslims routinely approach "reason," "human rights," "equality," and the like not as constructs assiduously gleaned from Muslim scripture or tradition, nor as abstract, neutral values or principles in and of themselves. Rather, these concepts are routinely understood and pursued in the form of very specific and storied Western concretions. For example, Islam's allowance of polygyny is condemned as wrong or unacceptable because it violates the principles of human rights and equality.[40] The remedy, however, is never sought in Muslim re-interpretations of Islamic law or scripture that simply sanction polyandry.[41] For while allowing polyandry might render Muslim women equal to

39. See his classic, *Moral Man and Immoral Society* (New York: Charles Schribner's Sons, 1960), xxiii. This was a reprint of the work that first appeared in 1932.

40. See, e.g., A. An-Na'īm, "Sharī'ah and Basic Human Rights Concerns," *Liberal Islam*, ed. C. Kurzman (New York: Oxford University Press, 1998), 232–233.

41. This is not an argument in favor of polyandry but an attempt to show how its status, among many modern Muslims, like that of numerous other "controversial issues," is more informed by the storied sensibilities of the non-Muslim West than it is by Muslim scripture or tradition. Of course, it might be argued that the sources of Islam, along with its legal and

Muslim men (in terms of their equal right to multiple partners), it is not likely to make Islam equal to the ascending West. Again, however, the issue here is not whether such re-readings *could* be vindicated on the basis of interpretive approaches and substantive considerations internal to Islam. The issue is, rather, whether such re-interpretations *are* ultimately motivated by a preconscious, undisciplined desire for acceptance and validation or by a principled, good-faith commitment to God.

Of course, the whole notion of whether a Muslim is honestly committed to God is tied in one way or another to his or her perceived level of adherence to Islamic "law" (*fiqh, sharī'ah*) and theology (*'ilm al-kālām, 'aqīdah*). Yet, as *rational* disciplines, both Islamic "law" and theology are susceptible to the dictates of preconscious, prerational motivators. As the great al-Ghazālī (d. 505/1111) reminded us as far back as the sixth/twelfth century: "Reason is merely a guide, while impulses and motives issue from the self (*al-nafs*)."[42] In the West, Thomas Hobbes (d. 1679) would later confirm: "Thoughts

exegetical tradition, are simply too univocally stacked against polyandry for this to be a feasible option. I agree. But one might say the same about homosexuality, *ribā* (interest?), the shares of inheritance or prescribed criminal sanctions (ḥudūd). Yet, all of these have been the target of attempts at reinterpretation. On homosexuality, see S. S. Kugle, "Sexuality, Diversity, and Ethics in the Agenda of Progressive Muslims," *Progressive Muslims: On Justice, Gender and Pluralism*, ed. O. Safi (Oxford: Oneworld, 2003), 190–234; *Homosexuality in Islam: Critical Reflections on Gay, Lesbian and Transgender Muslims* (Oxford: Oneworld, 2010); on *ribā*, see Abdullah Saeed, *Islamic Banking and Interest: A Study of the Prohibition of Riba and Its Contemporary Interpretation* (Leiden: E.J. Brill, 1997); on the shares of inheritance, see W. B. Hallaq (treating the Syrian, Muhammad Shahrur's reform methodology), *A History of Islamic Legal Theories: An Introduction to Sunni Uṣūl al-Fiqh* (Cambridge: Cambridge University Press, 1999), 245–253; on prescribed criminal punishments (apostasy), see M. H. Kamali, *Freedom of Expression in Islam* (Cambridge: Islamic Texts Society, 1997), 92–98; T. J. 'Alwānī, *Lā ikrāha fī al-dīn: ishkālīyat al-riddah wa al-murtaddīn min ṣadr al-islām ilā al-yawm* (Cairo: Maktabat al-Shurūq al-Dawlīyah, 1427/2006).

42. See Abū Ḥāmid al-Ghazālī, *al-Mustaṣfā min 'ilm al-uṣūl*, 2 vols. ed. M. 'Abd al-Shakūr (Būlāq: al-Maṭba'ah al-Amīrīyah, 1322/1904), 1: 61.

are to the Desires, as Scouts and Spies, to range abroad, and find the way to the things desired . . . The mind is moved by desire, the active element of the self."[43] While law and theology are thus the primary means through which Muslims gauge religiosity and pursue the public validation of feelings, beliefs, or actions, neither is immune to the subtle machinations of the self and thus to serving as the object rather than the overseer of preconscious passions.[44] Nor, more importantly, does it fall within the mandate of law or theology per se to penetrate and direct the preconscience through the psychodynamic instantiation of the kinds of beliefs, sensibilities, decisions, or motivations that result in God-pleasing acts and states of being. Rather, this concern has typically, even if not exclusively,[45] fallen to the masters and discipline of Sufism or *taṣawwuf*.

43. Cited in R. M. Unger, *Knowledge and Politics* (New York: The Free Press, 1975), 37–38. As I have suggested elsewhere, however (e.g., *Islam and the Problem of Black Suffering*, 10), what is generally referred to as "reason" is not the plain, unmediated dictates of the human faculties but a highly contested result of historically informed, corporate attempts to deploy these in a formally systematic way. As Hans-Georg Gadamer put the matter, "Reason exists for us only in concrete historical terms, i.e., it is not its own master, but remains constantly dependent on the given circumstances in which it operates." See his "The History of Understanding," in *The Hermeneutics Reader*, ed. K. Mueller-Vollmer (New York: Continuum Publishing Company, 1985), 260. Meanwhile, L. S. Mudge and J. N. Poling express a similar notion, in *Formation and Reflection: The Promise of Practical Theology* (Minneapolis, MN: Fortress Press, 2009), xix: "We are conditioned from birth to the world view of our surroundings. Cognitive powers are programmed or coded below the level of consciousness. 'Reason' is a product of socialization, from the oedipal resolution to graduate school and beyond."
44. On this theme, see the critique by al-Ghazālī in my *On the Boundaries of Theological Tolerance in Islam: Abū Ḥāmid al-Ghazālī's Fayṣal al-Tafriqa* (New York: Oxford University Press, 2002), 87–88, where he speaks of jurists and theologians, "whose god (*ilāh*) is their undisciplined passions (*hawā*), whose object of worship (*maʿbūd*) is their leaders, whose direction of prayer (*qibla*) is the *dīnār*, whose religious law is their own frivolity, whose will (*irāda*) is the promotion of reputation and carnal pleasures, whose worship (*ʿibāda*) is the service they render the rich among them, whose remembrance (of God) is the devilish whisperings of their souls, whose most cherished possession is their (relationship with their) political leaders, and whose every thought is preoccupied with extracting legal dodges (*ḥiyal*/s. *ḥīla*) to accommodate the dictates of their (would-be) sense of shame."
45. In the Western tradition the tendency is to equate all spiritual enterprises in Islam with Sufism, whether the practitioners of these would do so or not and whether or not Muslims

a. Sufism: Between Mysticism and Personal Piety

It is precisely here, however, that we come to what has evolved into a major, modern ideological impasse among Muslims. Simply stated, many Muslims find such descriptions of *taṣawwuf* to be too charitable if not intentionally misleading in their underinclusiveness. For, while acknowledging that the early Muslim spiritual progenitors were committed to ascetic practices aimed at aligning the human will with divine pleasure, they would insist (in agreement with a significant body of Western scholarship) that full-blown Sufism took a decidedly mystical turn.[46] In fact, so central would mystical concerns become to the Sufi enterprise that after the word "Sufism" itself—which is more a transliteration than a translation—the most common scholarly rendering of *taṣawwuf* today is simply

---

more generally might identify other modes and thrusts of spiritual labor and purification. In reality, however, even modern opponents of Sufism, e.g., Salafis in general, are not opposed to "spirituality" per se and remain committed to refining and purifying the self. In fact, "purification of the self," i.e., *tazkīyat al-nafs, sulūk*, plays as central a role in many expressions of Salafism as it does in Sufism. In such light, it seems unfair and erroneous to imply that Salafi opposition to Sufism necessarily entails opposition to "spirituality." Nor is non-Sufi (to be distinguished from anti-Sufi) spirituality a purely modern phenomenon. Rather, one can go all the way back to the likes of Aḥmad b. Ḥanbal and move forward to the likes of Ibn Ḥazm, Ibn al-Jawzī, Ibn Qayyim al-Jawzīyah, Ibn Taymīya, and others. Sufism, meanwhile, might be distinguished by the greater leeway it grants to religious imagination, which, at least from the perspective of its opponents, may be its greatest liability. At any rate, as we will see in discussing Ibn Taymīya below, Sufi and non-Sufi approaches to self-purification are not necessarily mutually exclusive or mutually opposed to each other.

46. See, e.g., C. Melchert, "The transition from asceticism to mysticism at the middle of the ninth century C.E.," *Studia Islamica* vol. 83 no. 1 (1996) 51–70. It is important to note in this context Melchert's explicit observation: "Of course, ascetical single-mindedness never left Islam, or even (*pace* al-Dhahabī) Sufism." See "Transition," 62 nt. 68. This would certainly be borne out by the case of such later Sufis as those described by A. T. Karamustafa in *God's Unruly Friends: Dervish Groups in the Later Islamic Middle Period, 1200–1550* (Salt Lake City: University of Utah Press, 1994). Indeed, Karamustafa depicts these groups as part of a "renunciatory movement" whose "various manifestations forged the features of poverty, mendicancy, itinerancy, celibacy, self-mortification, and other forms of social deviance into distinct combinations with varying degrees of emphasis on the eremitic and cenobitic options." *God's Unruly Friends*, 3.

"mysticism."[47] "Mysticism," however, is dedicated first and foremost not so much to *serving* God as it is to *enjoying* God, that is, to perfecting not the worship of God but rather the ecstatic experience of God, from the simple, innate perception of God's immanent presence to actual feats of apotheosis and pantheistic union.[48] In this light, many would insist, to describe Sufism as simply an effort to penetrate and redirect the preconscience toward the heteronomous service and worship of God is to engage in something on the order of propaganda.

47. See, e.g., Annmarie Schimmel, *Mystical Dimensions of Islam* (Chapel Hill, NC: University of North Carolina Press, 1978); P. Awn, "Sufism," *The Encyclopedia of Religion*, 16 vols. ed. M. Eliade (New York: Macmillan Publishing Company, 1987), 14: 104: "One of the truly creative manifestations of religious life in Islam is the mystical tradition, known as Sufism." W. Chittick objects to the use of "mysticism," but his reasons for this do not appear to be fully consistent. See his *Faith and Practice of Islam: Three Thirteenth Century Sufi Texts* (New York: State University of New York Press, 1992), 168ff. On the one hand, in order to avoid certain negative connotations that have accrued to "mysticism" in Western discourse, he intimates that mysticism is marginal to Sufism. Indeed, he insists, "Much more central to Sufism's concerns are discipline, training, control of the instinctive urges of the self, achievement of a balanced psyche, overcoming mental and moral weakness, virtue, piety, devotion, avoidance of sin, and so on." (p. 170) Still, Chittick affirms, "Without question, direct and intimate knowledge of God plays an important role in Sufism." (p.169) In fact, he insists, so central is this "direct and intimate knowledge of God" that, because they never attain it, "the vast majority of people affiliated with Sufism are not Sufis"! (p. 169)
48. While there are several, competing (and thus no single, universally recognized) definition of mysticism, all appear to unite in the common commitment to immediate contact and direct experience of God. See, e.g., *A Dictionary of Religions*, ed. J. R. Hinnels (Oxford: Blackwell Publishers, Ltd., 1995), 333: "*Mysticism*, In theistic traditions often described as a fundamental unitive experience of love and communion with God." See also *Encyclopedia of Religion* 2nd ed., ed. L. Jones (Detroit: Macmillan Reference USA, 2005), 6341–6342. While, on the one hand, it is affirmed that there is no single definition that could accommodate all mystical experience, it is also asserted that, "Mysticism belongs to the core of all religion . . . [a]ll religions, regardless of their origin, retain their vitality only as long as their members continue to believe in a transcendent reality with which they can in some way communicate by direct experience." See also I. Marcoulesco, "Mystical Union," *The Encyclopedia of Religion*, 16 vols. ed. M. Eliade (New York: Macmillan Publishing Company, 1987), 10: 240: "All types of mysticism culminate in some form of *unitive* experience, perceived as either internal or external unity." (Italics original.)

In addition to these first-order mystical concerns, there are second-order aspects of (especially later) Sufism that challenge its image as benign spiritual training. There is its institutional side with its often rigid and in some instances cult-like hierarchy between master and disciple. Especially in its more popular forms, there is the tendency toward crass superstition and an overindulgence of the belief in the Sufi master's omniscience or ability to effect supernatural extractions of service from nature, in the form of miracles or intercessions with the divine. All of this is accompanied, moreover, by a semantically supple if not promiscuous Sufi lexicon and a marked preference for processing, articulating, and augmenting understandings of reality and revelation not simply through the publicly owned and corporately regulated medium of reason but the more private and less easily monitored faculty of religious imagination. On these tendencies, Sufism is seen by many modern Muslims, especially those of a more conservative[49] or reformist bent, not simply as a complement to law and theology but as a potential threat to and contradiction of them.[50]

Law and theology embrace exotericism and demand, in theory at least, that truth-claims be backed by objective (that is, publicly accessible and demonstrable) proof (*dalīl*/pl. *adillah*). Sufism, on

49. The designation "conservative" as applied to Muslims today takes on certain negative associations, particularly with violence and intolerance, which I do not intend by its use here. Rather, by "conservative" I have in mind something closer to Michael Oakeshott's description of the term: "to prefer the familiar to the unknown, to prefer the tried to the untried, fact to mystery, the actual to the possible, the limited to the unbounded, the near to the distant, the sufficient to the superabundant, the convenient to the perfect, the present laughter to utopian bliss. . . ." See M. Oakeshott, "On Being Conservative" in *Rationalism in Politics and Other Essays* (Indianapolis: Liberty Fund, Inc., 1991), 408–409.

50. These are quite common critiques and observations that go back to the end of the nineteenth and beginning of the twentieth century. See, for example, the many inquiries and responses, including some that go back to Ibn Taymīya, cited by Muḥammad Rashīd Riḍā in *al-Manār: 1898–1935*, 37 vols. (Cairo: *Maṭbaʿat al-Manār*, N.d.), 9: 852–855; 24: 218–226; 24: 273–279; 24: 508–519; 27: 748–754, and passim.

the other hand, has from early on recognized if not privileged esotericism, openly admitting the authority of such individualistic, subjective epistemes as intuitive taste (*dhawq*), spiritual insight (*baṣīrah*), mystical unveiling (*kashf*), oneiric epiphanies (*ru'yā*/pl. *ru'an*), and supersensory knowledge (*ma'rifah*). While these have been known to contribute to any number of sober realizations (as, for example, with al-Ghazālī's spiritual recovery), they have also been implicated in such startling excesses as Abū Yazīd al-Basṭāmī's (d. 234/848 or 261/875) declarations, "Glory be to me"; "Thy obedience to me is greater than my obedience to Thee"; "I am I, and there is no God but I";[51] "There is nothing in this garment but God";[52] or the more famous, if no less shocking, utterance by Ḥusayn b. Manṣūr al-Ḥallāj (d. 309/922): "I am The Truth (*anā al-ḥaqq*)."[53] Clearly, there is much more at work here than the mere attempt to subjugate the passions and perfect the heteronomous worship of God. And clearly, without the salutary complement of law and theology, Sufism may be equally susceptible to the appetitive ravages of the preconscious self.

To be fair, however, as I have suggested elsewhere,[54] such articulations hardly represented the whole of Sufism, not even Sufism-as-mysticism. In fact, depending on time and place, these kinds of public outbursts might be considered exceptional if not idiosyncratic.[55] Postclassical Sufism of the fifth to sixth/eleventh to twelfth centuries, however, did develop and proceed on a conception of God that was essentially, to use the description of Alexander Knysh,

51. See A. Knysh, *Islamic Mysticism*, 71.
52. See Melchert, "Transition," 58.
53. Knysh, *Islamic Mysticism*, 75.
54. See my *Islam and the Blackamerican*, 175, 193–194.
55. Knysh notes, for example, that al-Basṭāmī was a loner who did not represent any particular Sufi group. See *Islamic Mysticism*, 69.

"monistic," that is, it reflected the notion that God is not simply the only efficient cause but the only actual reality in existence.[56] This would introduce its own set of challenges and open a new chapter in the polemic around *taṣawwuf*. Given the clear theological and moral implications of this "monistic" thrust ("If all is God, all is good and nothing is either evil or nondivine"), this development would be met with formidable scrutiny and almost *ad nauseam* attack, most especially by the redoubtable Ḥanbalite Traditionalist Taqī al-Dīn Ibn Taymīya (d. 728/1328). While Ibn Taymīya took issue, however, with antinomian, pantheistic, and theologically syncretic expressions of Sufism, not to mention the excesses of some of its more popular forms, he recognized and appreciated the positive pietistic thrust of the early centuries and some of Sufism's greatest representatives. Thus, in the aggregate, his writings reflect a palpable commitment to avoiding overinclusive judgments about Sufism. At one point, for example, he writes of the Sufis:

> The corrupt doctrines and practices that have infected these people have caused some groups to reject the way of the Sufis altogether, root and branch, such that those who veer from the proper course in this regard fall into two groups: 1) a group that accepts both what is true and what is false of the Sufi way; and 2) a group that rejects both what is true and what is false of the Sufi way, such as many groups of theologians and jurists. And the right position is simply to accept of this way, as well as any other way, that which is consistent with the Book and Sunna, and to reject of it, as well as other ways, that which violates the Book and Sunna.[57]

56. See Knysh, *Islamic Mysticism*, 170.
57. Ibn Taymīya, *al-Tuḥfah al-irāqīyah fī al-a'māl al-qalbīyah* (Cairo: al-Maṭba'ah al-Salafīyah wa Maktabatuhā, 1386/1966), 83. In fact, in line with this notion that whoever bases his or her view on truth is to be recognized for such, Ibn Taymīya even invokes the authority

Despite such efforts, however—indeed, despite his numerous writings on the subject and even his formal association with the Qādirī Sufi order[58]—Ibn Taymīya would ultimately come to be viewed as the archenemy of Sufism. By the twentieth century, this image would be joined and its impact reinforced by various modernizing and antimodernizing critiques of *taṣawwuf* by conservative and liberal religious reformers, secular nationalists, and Western-educated elites. All of these would ultimately fall against a backdrop of certain tendencies toward a rationalist fundamentalism spawned by aspects or understandings of the European Enlightenment(s). As a result, despite its often facile and overinclusive nature, much of the contemporary bias against *taṣawwuf* would simply blend into the tapestry of modern "sense," where it would be internalized as "normal," "reasonable," "educated," or simply "modern." In the end, this would place much of the criticism of Sufism beyond objective analysis and critique.

To be sure, however, facile argumentation and misrepresentation were not and are not the exclusive preserve of the critics of Sufism. In their effort to vindicate various forms and aspects of Sufism-as-mysticism, proponents of *taṣawwuf* also engage in what appears to be

---

of the aforementioned al-Basṭāmī as proof of the validity of his perspective on intercession and seeking supernatural assistance (*istighāthah*) from other than God: "And of this genre is the statement of Abū Yazīd al-Basṭāmī, 'A created being's seeking the supernatural assistance of another created being is like a drowning person seeking the assistance of another drowning person.'" See "*al-Istighāthah*" in *Majmū'at al-rasā'il al-kubrā*, 2 vols. (Cairo: Maktabat wa Maṭba'at Muḥammad 'Alī Ṣubayḥ wa Awlādih, N.d), 1: 485.

58. On this point see G. Makdisi, "Ibn Taimīya: A Sufi of the Qādirīya Order," *American Journal of Arabic Studies* 1 (1973): 118–129. 'Abd al-Qādir al-Jīlānī (d. 561/1166), founder of the Qādirī order, has been associated with an emphasis on "the moral and ethical aspects of Sufi piety." (Knysh, *Islamic Mysticism*, 171) Indeed, he is said to have "carefully avoided the metaphysical speculations that were advanced by some contemporary Sufi theorists and played down the sensational and individualistic aspects of mystical experience exemplified by al-Bisṭāmī and al-Ḥallāj." See Knysh, *Islamic Mysticism*, 181.

a willful blurring of the boundary between its pietistic and its mystical dimensions. Rather than defend, in other words, on substantive grounds, the apparently pantheistic mystical creeds of Muḥyī al-Dīn Ibn ʿArabī (d. 638/1240) or Jalāl al-Dīn al-Rūmī (d. 672/1273), defenders of *taṣawwuf* often attempt to insulate these through vague and general vindications of Sufism as a whole, casting it as the simple commitment to "pietistic self-purification" (*tazkīyah*) or plain old "religious perfectionism" (*iḥsān*). Of course, the ultimate aim of this conflation is to thwart all criticism of Sufism as such and to reinforce this via the subtle insinuation that to criticize *taṣawwuf* at all is to criticize spirituality and spiritual refinement in favor of a stale, "legalistic," spiritually hollow form of religiosity. Rather than convince its opponents, however, this approach more often than not simply reduces them to a bitter acquiescence that merely masks their suspicion of Sufism as a Trojan horse bearing all manners of theological and practical impropriety.[59] In the end, while opponents of Sufism press their case by equating *taṣawwuf* with mysticism[60]—pantheistic, antinomian mysticism at that!— defenders of Sufism are equally guilty of conflating it with simple pietism, in order to mask the various mystical, theological, and practical shenanigans that some Sufis have been known to practice and endorse.[61]

59. This is not to mention the suspicion that Sufism is often invoked not as a complement but as an alternative to orthodox law and theology and that Sufism-as-mysticism, at least in some forms, completely marginalizes the concern with personal piety, not to mention social justice, as expressed through standard régimes of religious observance.

60. It should be clear that my objection here is not to "mysticism" as a rendering of Sufism. My point is simply that the various forms of mystical experience advocated by various Sufis makes Sufism-as-mysticism an easy target for overinclusive detractors.

61. Representative of this trend are perhaps S. Murata and W. Chittick, who, on the one hand, object to the use of "mysticism" as a translation for Sufism and refer to it instead as "a manifestation of *iḥsān*," which itself is said to revolve around "the rectification of character." See *The Vision of Islam* (New York: Paragon Books, 1994), 238, 304. Meanwhile, in the interstices of their actual discussion on *iḥsān*, we read such statements as, "To be fully human is

The upshot of all of this is a vague but extremely operative diffidence if not paralysis among many modern Muslims, especially in the United States, toward Sufism as a whole, *including* its nonmystical, nonpantheistic, pietistic psychology of moral and devotional rectitude. As a result, especially for those who are devoid or distrustful of mystical inclinations, Sufism's contributions to the enterprise of spiritual refinement, taming the prerational self and inculcating internally driven religiosity is placed beyond the pale of what many modern Muslims feel they can indulge in good conscience, the proverbial baby being thrown out with the bathwater. On this constriction, Islamic law and theology are routinely left to the disposal of the unrefined, prerational self, "to range abroad, and find the way to the things desired."[62] This in a world, moreover, where palpable disparities with "the West"—in power, authority, the ability to craft and disseminate images, sensibilities, and ideals—continue to stoke powerful, preconscious impulses toward modes of rejection, accommodation, or dissociation that can only be indulged through a conscious (or perhaps at times not so conscious) flouting or misappropriation of God's will.

The Bride-Groom's Crown goes a long way in addressing, and indeed, assuaging, many of these concerns. *Pace* the liberal assumption that sin and evil can be ultimately traced to social institutions, ignorance, bad experiences, or environment, Ibn 'Aṭā' Allāh recognizes that, on its own and even in a perfect state of nature, the human self (*nafs*) can play an adversarial role and come between one and the universe of values and meanings that lead to God. On this recognition, *The Bride-Groom's Crown* directs attention to the

to actualize the divine form" (p. 304); "Created in the form of God, they contain within themselves all God's attributes, but only latently or mutedly" (p. 308); "The 'bodily resurrection' is not only a dogma in Islam, it is also the only possible way to explain how people can be divine and human at the same time." (p. 317)

62. "We worship God by loathing America."

self *qua* self and includes a moving contribution to the inculcation and protection of God-consciousness, personal piety, and the primacy of internally driven religiosity. At the same time, however, Ibn 'Aṭā' Allāh recognizes that humans do not exist in a state of nature but in a state of society, as a result of which self-refinement must include a coming to terms with various social, cultural, and other externals in a manner that informs the very meaning and mechanics of spiritual struggle. Finally, by downplaying mysticism—especially its pantheistic tendencies—and avoiding many of the sensitivities that Sufi works in general are known to aggravate among non-Sufis, *The Bride-Groom's Crown* goes a long way in salvaging the personal piety side of Sufism from the purgatory to which the ideologically driven heaves and shoves of the friends and foes of Sufism-as-mysticism have ultimately condemned it.

IV. *THE BRIDE-GROOM'S CROWN*: SEMINAL THEMES AND SENSIBILITIES

Essentially a work of religious aphorisms, *The Bride-Groom's Crown* does not proceed in a consistent, topically organized fashion; rather, it drifts back and forth in a manner almost suggestive of a stream-of-consciousness mood. This discursive quality is joined by Ibn 'Aṭā' Allāh's conspicuous indulgence of religious imagination, as opposed to restricting himself to the plain faculty of reason. Along with the vastness of the array of issues it addresses, this makes it virtually impossible to summarize the contents of this text. There is, however, a number of seminal themes and sensibilities whose elucidation might prove useful in guiding one's reading of the text.

The Bride-Groom's Crown is explicit in its emphasis on Sufism's psychology of devotional rectitude. The cultivation and preservation of internally driven piety easily take up the bulk of the text. Page after page, Ibn 'Aṭā' Allāh exhorts his reader to guard the sanctity of the heart, beware of the treachery and beguilements of the self, and be mindful of the paradoxically fragile yet invincible nature of one's relationship with God and the eschatological implications of mortality. This is all interspersed with practical insight and instruction, from the importance of observing silence to limiting one's intake of food, from minding the company one keeps to the futility of relying upon one's faculties alone.

Its reliance on aphorism and religious imagination notwithstanding, *The Bride-Groom's Crown* is not an antireason tract. On the contrary, Ibn 'Aṭā' Allāh counts reason among God's most precious gifts to humans. [¶285] Having recognized this, however, he remains unconvinced that reason alone can tame or regulate the self. In fact, given his recognition of the power of the prerational and reason's tendency to follow rather than lead desire, he sees reason as being just as susceptible to being manipulated by the self as the self is to being contained by reason. Indeed, he seems to doubt the existence of *any* form of reason that does not instinctively conceal, disguise or exploit the moral contradictions and compromises that permeate the prerational interests in whose behalf it operates.[63] What is needed, therefore, is an aid or complement to reason, as well as a check upon it. And Ibn 'Aṭā' Allāh locates this in a combination of confessional self-reflection, inspirational and humbling human experience, and unspoiled religious imagination. These, alongside a humble commitment to the religious law and following the example of the Prophet, become the means through which he

63. Compare, e.g., S. Jarvis, *Adorno: A Critical Reader* (New York: Routledge, 1988), 1–2: "What is the relationship between power and rationality. Can there ever be a kind of thinking which does not live off the suffering of others, or which does not suppress or conceal the injustices which it lives off?"

seeks to promote a deeper, more honest, and more mindful relationship with God. And this more mindful relationship with God becomes the key to self-refinement.

Self-reflection, human experience and religious imagination, however, are not limited to the individual but extend to the insights, discoveries, and tried and tested successes and failures of the Community as a whole. In fact, much of *The Bride-Groom's Crown* appears to be a summary of the nascent Shādhilī wisdom-tradition. Here, Ibn 'Aṭā' Allāh challenges the liberal tendency to isolate individuals as autonomous, unstoried subjects and effectively imputes to every Muslim a moral and devotional repertoire that is grounded in community that extends over space and time and connects the living to the dead and unborn. This is clearly the implication behind his frequent allusions to the trials and triumphs not only of bygone sages and masters but of anonymous, unsung devotional heroes and heroines as well.

The Bride-Groom's Crown begins with the theme of repentance (*tawbah*) and insists that nothing else matters in the absence of this. [¶12] This helps set the practical and anti-utopian tone of the work. On the one hand, it introduces self-refinement as a practical enterprise, fundamentally grounded in a concrete commitment to spiritual labor. At the same time, it underscores the fact that, for Ibn 'Aṭā' Allāh, every attempt to turn religion into a factory for producing "moral robots" or "perfect societies" ever so subtly distorts if not undermines religion. So too does the utopian vision of every antireligious secular absolutist and every would-be self-assured (and often overly self-assuring) religious fundamentalist. For such instrumentalizations invariably devalue religion in proportion to the number of religious followers who continue to exist as flawed human beings. Yet, flawed humans, sincerely struggling—sometimes successfully, sometimes not—to remember and fulfill a cosmic debt to an ultimately ineffable

God is the very essence of Islam.[64] And it is ultimately the quality of this remembrance, the persistence of this struggle and the tenacity of this relationship—not simple success at behaving morally!— that constitutes the core of Muslim religiosity.[65]

While repentance, however, is Ibn 'Aṭā' Allāh's practical point of departure, his conceptual beginning is his simultaneous commitment to the twin principles of divine sovereignty and cosmic debt. For Ibn 'Aṭā' Allāh, human life, like the world that humans inhabit, is a gift. As such, the true ground of moral and devotional rectitude is not simply autonomous right reason but a psychodynamic recognition of a cosmic debt of gratitude to God. This explains his persistent use of such terms as "sin" (*dhanb*) and, especially, "disobedience" (*ma'ṣīyah*), as opposed to "evil" (*sharr*) or simply "unethical" (*qabīḥ*). For his

64. One is reminded here of a point made by Chris Hedges: "The concept of sin is a stark acknowledgment that we can never be omnipotent, that we are bound and limited by human flaws and self-interest. The concept of sin is a check on the utopian dreams of a perfect world. It prevents us from believing in our own perfectibility or the illusion that the material advances of science or technology equal an intrinsic moral improvement in our species." See his *I Don't Believe in Atheists* (New York: The Free Press, 2008), 14. Of course, Ibn 'Aṭā' Allāh, especially as an Ash'arite, would part with Hedges on the notion that the concept of sin can survive independent of belief in God. On the Ash'arite implications here, see my *Islam and the Problem of Black Suffering*, 83–85.

65. Underscoring this anti-utopian thrust, none other than the reputedly puritanical Ibn Taymīya is fond of citing the Prophetic report narrated by al-Bukhārī of a man named Ḥumār who used to humor the Prophet but who also had a love affair with the grape, as a result of which he would repeatedly get drunk, get caught, and be punished. One day, after punishing him, the Companions proceeded to curse him for his recidivism. At this, the Prophet interjected, "Do not curse him. For, verily, he loves God and he loves His Messenger." See Ibn Taymīya, *al-Tuḥfah al-'irāqīyah fī al-a'māl al-qalbīyah* (Cairo: al-Maṭba'ah al-Salafīyah wa Maktabatuhā, 1386/1966), 39. There are other well-known hadith in this regard, such as that depicting a man and a prostitute whose transgressions will be forgiven by God because of their charitable gesture toward a dog suffering severe thirst. See Muslim b. Ḥajjāj, *Ṣaḥīḥ muslim*, 4: 1405 (*Kitāb al-salām*). On the other hand, there are hadith depicting persons who persist in prima facie morally upright behavior, such as learning and teaching the Qur'ān, fighting jihad and giving charity, only to end up in Hell. See, e.g., the hadith to this effect narrated by al-Bukhārī and cited by Ibn Taymīya in *al-Tuḥfah al-'irāqīyah*, 63.

primary concern lies not with violations of rationally deduced morality or conventional ethics but with misalignments between the human will and the divine command. Obedience and disobedience, moreover, are not simply modes of *acting* but also of *being*. Thus, even when one is not engaged in concrete physical action per se, remembering God (*dhikr*) and one's cosmic debt remains a priority. Ultimately, Ibn 'Aṭā' Allāh insists, the true ground of this "psychological obedience" is trust in God. Indeed, he states, "The most beloved manifestation of obedience to God is trust in Him." [¶147]

Though Ibn 'Aṭā' Allāh's morality goes beyond formal ethical principles (for example, Kant's categorical imperative) and social conventions (for example, saying, "Please" and "Thank you"), this does not mean that he sees a contradiction between being a "good person" and having a proper relationship with God. He does, however, want to discourage the tendency to see the former as necessarily entailing the latter. To this end, he asks rhetorically and answers matter-of-factly: "Do you think that good character is simply for a person to be pleasant? One who honors people but tramples upon the rights of God* does not have good character."[¶214] Again, this speaks to the fact that Ibn 'Aṭā' Allāh's point of departure is not a grand vision of the "good society," but a humble, almost nagging, heteronomous recognition of a cosmic debt to God.

Piety, however, and one's ability to honor one's debt to God are not the only interests affected by sin and disobedience. Rather, the entire constellation of one's powers of perception and realization are affected as well. As Ibn 'Aṭā' Allāh describes it, disobedience brings down darkness upon a person, blackening their heart and lowering over them a veil that stands between them and God. Indeed, it is in this broader context that the self, *al-nafs*, as the seat of preconscious, undisciplined passion, comes to be seen as an impediment not only to the practical expression of rightly constituted religiosity but to overall human potential as well. For the self knows naturally and pursues instinctively only what it deems to be good or serviceable to it, not its host. And left unchecked, its desires can take on the status of absolute good, at which time its ultimate ambition comes to reside in colonizing the person. In this capacity, the self will oppose all values, meanings and commitments that threaten to thwart its efforts at self-fulfillment, including—and perhaps especially—those values, meanings, and commitments that bind one to God.

While the passion-seeking self may be a motivator of sin, disobedience, and misperception, passion itself is not limited to such carnal desires as food and sex. To be sure, these are major players, but they do not capture the full sense of what Ibn 'Aṭā' Allāh has in mind when he focuses on the problem of carnal desire, "*shahwah*," or its cognate, undisciplined passion, "*hawā*." As humans exist not in a state of nature but in a state of society, any number of intangible, nonsensual, socially informed desires and passions—from the passion for fame and preeminence, to the desire for acceptance and the avoidance of criticism, to the passion for love or revenge—can promote sin, disobedience, and misperception if left unrefined. Thus, even if one completely avoids the temptations of the "two repositories," that is, the mouth and the genitals, one may remain a prisoner of *shahwah* or *hawā* and thus in a continued state of moral *cum*-devotional dereliction. Earlier, his teacher, al-Shādhilī had identified these nonsensual animators as "barely perceptible desires" (*shahwah khafīyah*),[66] identifying as a concrete example of such "the undisciplined desire to exact revenge from those who have wronged one."[67] Ibn 'Aṭā' Allāh goes on to

66. See al-Sha'rānī, *Ṭabaqāt*, 294. See also the text and commentary of *Ḥikam ibn 'aṭā' Allāh*, 40, where both Ibn 'Aṭā' Allāh and Aḥmad Zarrūq speak of the "barely perceptible desires."
67. Al-Sha'rānī, *Ṭabaqāt*, 294.

intimate in *The Bride-Groom's Crown* that even the assiduous pursuit of religious knowledge can ultimately add up to little more than a "barely perceptible desire." [¶112]

On this understanding, even consistently observed prayer, fasting, and avoidance of illicit sex and alcohol might not negate the fact that one who utters a statement such as, "We worship Allah by loathing America," remains in the throes of an unrefined self and its undisciplined passions. So too would one who sought to bargain away God's legislative prerogative in exchange for recognition by the dispensers of quotidian validation. Given the power and subtlety of "barely perceptible desire," the road to compromise is often as dark as it is inexorable. As Ibn 'Aṭā' Allāh put it, one may begin as an ostensible devotee of God, as a result of which one earns the title, "servant of The Grand" (*'Abd al-Kabīr*). But this may soon degenerate into a barely perceptible desire for recognition or acceptance or revenge, on the strength of which one furtively bargains away one's religion and comes to be designated "the governor's pet" (*shaykh al-amīr*). [¶270]

To be sure, part of the difficulty here lies not simply with the presence of these passions per se but with the ease with which they can be disguised, sublated, and placed beyond recognition. In other words, the power or pervasiveness of the sociopolitical realities that animate these passions can imbue one with the sense that they are "natural," morally unquestionable, or a priori. Alternatively, the fact that one may be otherwise committed and habituated to a life of religious devotion can simply blind one to the presence and depth of "barely perceptible desires."[68] It is here, in this essentially agnostic engagement with forms of *shahwah* and *hawā* that do not attach to

68. See also Ibn Taymīya, who speaks of "barely perceptible desires" (*shahwah khafīyah*) and identifies them as a long-standing concern in Islam. He writes: "Many people harbor in their selves a latent love of preeminence of which they are not fully cognizant. On the

the senses, that God and religion become most susceptible to being deployed, perhaps at times even unwittingly, as tools in the employ of the self.

And yet, the solution to all of this is neither to kill all desires (including all barely perceptible ones) nor to mortify the self. The solution is, rather, to *refine* these by way of a proper relationship with God. As Ibn 'Aṭā' Allāh puts it, "Shut out the influence of people's gazing at you through your knowledge of God's gazing at you. And be oblivious to their advances by witnessing His." [¶249] Here, however, one must be careful not to mistake the menu for the meal; one must distinguish between God's law and God, on the one hand, and between theology or concepts *about* God and actual God, on the other. This is not to cast aspersions on the intrinsic value of law or theology. It is simply to warn against the possibility of mentally constructed abstractions *about* God or God's will coming between one and an actual relationship *with* God. Law, in other words, might define the boundaries of proper conduct; but even the assiduous observance of these should not be confused with a proper and genuine psychospiritual relationship with God. In a similar manner, theology might play an important role in guarding the God-human relationship against impropriety; but it should facilitate rather than hamper this relationship; and it should certainly not preempt it. In sum, law and theology may be conduits, vessels, or guardrails through which a proper relationship with God is pursued and manifested. But they themselves are not the actual foundation or ultimate ground of that relationship.

contrary, they are sincere in their worship, while their faults are barely perceptible to them. The scholarly discourse on this is wide and well-known. And they refer to this (problem) as 'barely perceptible desire' (*al-shahwah al-khafīyah*)." See Taqī al-Dīn Ibn Taymīya, *Majmū'at tafsīr shaykh al-islām ibn taymīya*, ed. 'A. Sharaf al-Dīn (Bombay: Dār al-Qayyimah, 1374/1954), 280.

According to Ibn ʿAṭāʾ Allāh, the ultimate foundation of this relationship is love.[69] And this is the key to refining the self. This is because the ultimate effect of love of God is to illuminate the inner being. And light is a far less hospitable forum than darkness in which to indulge impropriety and heedlessness. Moreover, even as this light provides voluntary disincentives to sin or disobey, it primes the self to find levels of satisfaction and discovery (that is, unveiling) that blunt the actual pleasures of sin and disobedience and open the way to levels of perception, understanding, and envisioning that lie beyond the more immediate appurtenances of the mundane world.

Having said all of this, Ibn ʿAṭāʾ Allāh is explicit in pointing out that this relationship with God is both organic, that is, subject to ebb and flow, and formal, that is, regulated by rules, principles, and even an etiquette, much like love in a marriage. To be sure, the source of this régime of propriety is the broad parameters of the religious law brought to practical perfection, according to Ibn ʿAṭāʾ Allāh, by the example of the Prophet. Here, however, the Prophetic example is presumed to guide not simply by conveying proper instruction but by actually inspiring in those who follow and imitate the Prophet what Edmund Burke might refer to as "proper prejudices," that is, not blind, stubborn habits of mind but proper prejudgments and prerational dispositions that provide direction even to those who lack the time or ability to trade wits with a quarrelsome, impassioned self.[70] Together, the religious law and Prophetic example mark the dividing line between genuine love for God and merely replacing

69. Here is another point, among many, on which Ibn ʿAṭāʾ Allāh and Ibn Taymīya agree. See the latter's *al-Tuḥfah al-ʿirāqīyah*, 62–63, 71–73, 84–85, and passim. Of course, the love theme is quite central to Sufism as a whole, going all the way back to the very early centuries and such luminaries as Rābiʿah al-ʿAdawīyah (d. 185/801), Sarī al-Saqaṭī (d. 253/867), and others.

70. Stanley Hauerwas expresses a similar concept in Christian terms: "Christian ethics involves learning to imitate another before it involves acting on principles (though principles are

one form of undisciplined passion with another. This is what Ibn 'Aṭā' Allāh has in mind when he states that, "God is not pleased by your state of loving Him but rather by your state of being loved by Him." [¶16] In other words, Ibn 'Aṭā' Allāh has no use for "spiritualized antinomianism." Nor, moreover, is he Gnostic in orientation. For him, self-refinement and all its benefits, including supersensory knowledge (*ma'rifah*), result not from crassly mortifying or transcending the flesh but from properly refining and disciplining it, as part of the cause and effect of establishing and sustaining a proper relationship with God.

To be sure, the self, its carnal passions and "barely perceptible desires" are powerful adversaries against which one must marshal all of one's powers. Still, Ibn 'Aṭā' Allāh is explicit in pointing out that material comforts in and of themselves are not the problem. Material comforts constitute a problem only to the extent that they serve as the goal for or means through which the undisciplined self enslaves its host. Otherwise, Ibn 'Aṭā' Allāh points out, the Companions of the Prophet included persons of the highest religious caliber, men such as Abū Bakr al-Ṣiddīq, 'Abd al-Raḥmān b. 'Awf, and others, who were extremely wealthy. [¶296–298]

In the end, Ibn 'Aṭā' Allāh recognizes that the path to self-refinement is a life-long enterprise that is fraught with difficulties, pitfalls, and disappointments. Here, however, in another expression of his anti-utopianism, he advises his readers not to give up, lose

not excluded)." "We do not become free by conforming our actions to the categorical imperative but by being accepted as disciples and thus learning to imitate a master . . . [M]orality is not chosen and then confirmed by the example of others; instead we learn what the moral life entails by imitating another." See his *The Hauerwas Reader* (Durham, NC: Duke University Press, 2001), 223, 225. Of course, the Muslim's ultimate master and object of imitation is the Prophet Muhammad, and this is ultimately what premodern Muslims were driving at with their reference to *al-ta'assī bi al-nabī*, "following the example of the Prophet as model."

hope, or be misled by the reality of their frailness as humans. On the contrary, when faced with the disappointment of moral *cum*-devotional failure and one's seeming inability to overcome it, one must simply repent. And when repentance itself seems to become so frequent as to be meaningless, Ibn 'Aṭā' Allāh insists, "The archer must continue to shoot. If he does not take home game today, he will take it tomorrow." [¶30] Indeed, against the urge to give up and simply surrender to the self, Ibn 'Aṭā' Allāh advises: "[D]o not be like the sick person who says, 'I will not treat my illness until I find the definitive cure.' For it will be said to you, 'You will not find the definitive cure until you commit to treating your illness.' There is no sweetness in jihad; there is but the jagged edges of swords. So prosecute the jihad against your self. That is the greatest jihad." [¶22]

In all of this, however, one must not become so taken with the power of one's faculties and achievements that one effectively comes to see these as a substitute for God. The key to avoiding the treacheries of the self resides neither in facile denials of its power nor in the sophomoric belief in the power of one's faculties alone to subdue it. Rather, one uses one's faculties and energies to enhance one's relationship with God; then one relies on God to direct, deliver, and sustain one. This is ultimately what Ibn 'Aṭā' Allāh has in mind when he takes up the issue of relying entirely on one's own comprehension and devices in planning one's life. The upshot of this discussion is that a proper relationship with God also implies a recognition of God's providential care for God's servants. On this belief, it is both folly and a contradiction of the relationship itself to imagine that one can care for oneself better than God can. This is not a call to abandon practical engagement or to flee from the challenges of sociopolitical reality. But if God is truly one's caretaker, one cannot imagine that one's own devices in repelling enemies or securing sustenance and social esteem can be superior to God's. On the contrary, obeying God and pursuing God's pleasure must always be a more effective means to happiness and security than obeying the dictates of the self in disobedience or obliviousness to God. This is the distinction Ibn 'Aṭā' Allāh has in mind when he speaks of "praiseworthy" versus "condemnable" planning, or "planning in competition with God." [¶283ff] Praiseworthy planning is planning that seeks to enhance one's relationship with God. Condemnable planning is planning that revolves around the self and its appetites, heedless of one's debt to God, as well as God's remunerative generosity and spontaneous grace.

In sum, sustaining a proper relationship with God and the universe of values and meanings that God imparts as an expression of God's normative preference is neither a purely rational enterprise nor one that humans can effectively sustain on their own. In fact, the very presumption that God's values, meanings, and preferences can be fully apprehended and safeguarded on the basis of reason alone assumes both that there is no distinction between divine "reason" and human reason and that divine prerogative could not separate what God might reasonably value from what God actually does value. Of course, it is precisely in this gap between what God could and does value that the unrefined self is able to enlist reason and all the rational enterprises (including law) into its cause. And it is only through divine guidance, mercy, and grace, mediated through a human will and pre-consciousness informed by its relationship with God, that this gap can be successfully managed, even if it can never be fully collapsed.

Ibn 'Aṭā' Allāh concludes *The Bride-Groom's Crown* with a mock address from God to God's servants and a personal address from Ibn 'Aṭā' Allāh to God. Again, given the aphoristic and richly imaginative nature of this work, this introduction could hardly exhaust its many, multilayered themes. It is my hope, however, that it does represent the most salient and seminal concerns and indications of the text.

V. THE TEXT AND THE TRANSLATION

There is little question that Ibn ʿAṭāʾ Allāh authored *The Bride-Groom's Crown,* as it appears on both lists of his works provided by Brockelmann.[71] I have relied on four printed editions as the basis of my translation. Of these, the most reliable is a Syrian edition edited by Muḥammad ʿAlī Muḥammad Baḥrī and Khālid Khādim al-Sarūjī and published by Ibn al-Qayyim press in Damascus in 1419/1999 (hereafter, *I.Q.*). The editors of *I.Q.* indicate that they relied on a manuscript held at the al-Asad library in Damascus (no. 7348, fols. 34–67), as well as four printed editions of the work, most directly one produced in Aleppo (whose date of publication they do not provide). They are generous in pointing out where they depart from the manuscript and often indicate their preference for what is in one of the printed editions.

The next most reliable among the editions I relied on was an old Cairene edition published by ʿAbbās ʿAbd al-Salām Shaqrūn press (hereafter, *Shaqrūn*) on the margins of Ibn ʿAṭāʾ Allāh's, *Kitāb al-Tanwīr fī Isqāṭ al-Tadbīr,* probably sometime during the first decade of the twentieth century. While there is wide agreement between the *Shaqrūn* and *I.Q.* editions, there are some differences, and *I.Q.*'s notes make it clear that the *Shaqrūn* edition was not among the printed copies its editors relied upon. *Shaqrūn* and *I.Q.* also appear to have relied on different manuscripts.

The third printed edition on which I relied was edited by ʿAbd al-Ghanī Nakah Mī and published by *Dār al-Kitāb al-Nafīs* in Aleppo in 1419/1999 (hereafter, *N.K.*). While this edition appears to agree

71. See *Geschichte,* II: 44, under the title, *Tāj al-ʿarūs wa qamʿ al-nufūs* (*The Bride-Groom's Crown on Subduing of the Self*); *Geschichte,* S II: 146, under the title *Tāj al-ʿarūs al-ḥāwī li tahdhīb al-nufūs wa qamʿ al-nufūs* (*The Bride-Groom's Crown Containing Instructions on Refining and Subduing the Self*).

in large measure with *I.Q.*, the editor gives no concrete information on the manuscripts or printed editions on which he relied. He adds section headings of his own, and at times appears to add emendations, placed between square brackets, without clearly explaining their source. There are also a number of added words and phrases that are unique to this edition and appear at times to be for the purpose of "guiding" the reader to a "proper" understanding of the text. I have tried to represent these additions as fully as deemed appropriate in the notes.

The fourth printed edition upon which I relied was edited by Muḥammad 'Abd al-Raḥmān 'Abd al-Jawwād al-Shāghūlī and published by *Dār Jawāmi' al-Kalim* in Cairo in 1425/2005. This edition (hereafter, *J.K.*) was based on a single manuscript in the Egyptian National Library, *Dār al-Kutub*, along with an unnamed printed edition. On the one hand, it does not appear to be as reliable as the above-mentioned editions. In fact, the editor (or his source) appears to fall into major fits of metathesis. On the other hand, one cannot entirely rule out the possibility that this was actually a related but separate work by Ibn 'Aṭā' Allāh, perhaps a reworking of *Tāj al-'Arūs* placed under a different title. Brockelmann lists a separate work under the title *al-Tuḥfah fī al-Taṣawwuf* (*A Collectible on Sufism*),[72] and this is actually the title under which al-Shāghūlī publishes the text. Still, there remain major segments of this edition that are exactly identical to the aforementioned editions of *The Bride-Groom's Crown*.

While I have taken *I.Q.* as the primary basis for my translation, I have not always agreed with its paragraphing and have imposed my own and numbered these for easy referencing. At times, one of the other editions will appear to be more reliable than *I.Q.*, in which case I will take it as my basis and indicate this in the notes. Between these

72. *Geschichte*, II: 144.

editions there are literally scores of variations, some minor, others less so. While it would be impractical to note all of these, I have tried to give a full accounting of those that might affect the translation or shed additional light on the manuscript tradition. All but *Shaqrūn* provide editorial notes, including information on the hadiths cited in the text. I have relied on and supplemented this information in an attempt to provide a full accounting of the hadiths adduced.

Regarding the translation itself, I should like to alert the reader to the following. First, classical Arabic is a highly elliptical language, especially in its literary form. Rather than cling slavishly, therefore, to a literal rendering and vex my reader with a plethora of brackets to represent my understanding of what is merely implied, I have chosen, with few exceptions, to lay out my understanding explicitly, as part of the text itself. Thus, for example, where the text reads, "*in qubila hādhā wa illā . . .*," my translation will read, "If this is accepted, all well and good; otherwise . . . ," without placing "all well and good" in brackets.

Second, Arabic often uses synonyms for stylistic or rhetorical effect. In order to avoid what may appear at times to be puerile redundancy, it may not always be suitable to maintain consistency in translating these into English. For example, in one place *makhāfah* will simply translate as "fear"; but where it appears in series with *khashyah*, that is, "godly fear," it will become "trepidation," in order to avoid such awkward redundancies as "godly fear and fear."

Third, while the avoidance of redundancy is a concern, there are a number of terms that I have taken to be technical terms in whose translation I have tried to remain consistent, even at the risk of redundancy. Thus, to take one example, *ghaflah* will appear as "heedlessness" throughout, even at the risk of awkwardness or repetition.

Fourth, also in the interest of avoiding a certain cumbersomeness in English, I have opted to substitute symbols for the various optatives and panegyrics, that is, (*) for *taʿālā* ("The Exalted"),

(*) for *ṣalla Allāhu 'alayhi wa sallama* ("God's peace and salutations be upon him"), (•) for *raḍiya Allāh 'anhu* ("May God be pleased with him"), and (°) for *raḥimahu Allāh* (May God have mercy on him).

Fifth, translating the full text of *The Bride-Groom's Crown* provided a broader context within which to understand and convey its meaning. This will explain, at least in part, those instances in which the present translation differs from the samplings I included in chapter 5 of *Islam and the Blackamerican*.

Finally, a word is in order about my rendering of *nafs*. In accordance with my understanding of Ibn 'Aṭā' Allāh, I have translated *nafs* almost exclusively as "self" and almost never as "soul," though it can also mean the latter and is plainly used in this sense in the Qur'ān, for example, "*kullu nafsin dhā'iqat al-mawt*" (*every soul shall taste death*). [3: 185, 21: 35, 29: 57] The reason for this rendering is that Ibn 'Aṭā' Allāh takes the *nafs* to be a problem and in so doing often casts it in a palpably negative light. My understanding of "self" in English is that it is more accommodating of negative connotations, as, for example, in our usage of the word "selfish." "Soul," on the other hand, tends more toward the positive, as with the word "soulful."

Given the nature, richness, and subject matter of *The Bride-Groom's Crown*, it is difficult to overcome the feeling that there remain countless ways in which my translation of this text could be improved, a feeling that never seemed to subside, despite my continued efforts at improvement. All in all, I have tried to combine the interests of accuracy, flow, and accessibility. And I have tried to be true to Ibn 'Aṭā' Allāh's tone or attitude toward his subject. In the end, as always, I can only hope, and this is my solemn prayer, that in my effort to introduce this text to the English-speaking world, my pen did not get the better of me and that I have compromised neither myself nor the great Sufi sage from Alexandria.

The Bride-Groom's Crown
Containing Instructions on Refining the Self

IBN 'AṬĀ' ALLĀH AL-SAKANDARI

Praise be to God, the Lord of all being and becoming. And may His salutations be upon our exemplar Muhammad, his family and Companions all. This is the book, *The Bride Groom's Crown Containing Instructions on Refining the Self*, by the Shaykh, Imam, and joiner of the two sciences, *sharīʿah* (which governs outward behavior) and *ḥaqīqah* (which addresses inner reality) Tāj al-Dīn Abū al-ʿAbbās Aḥmad b. 'Aṭā' Allāh al-Sakandarī, may God have mercy on him, grant him the ease and comfort of Paradise and cause the emanations of his grace to flow down upon us and upon all the Muslims. And may His blessings and salutations be upon our exemplar Muhammad and his Companions all. Amen.[1]

1. Much of this prolegomenon is missing from *J.K.*, 15, even according to the explicit colophon of the manuscript provided in the introduction to this edition. *N.K.*, 11, begins its edition with "*allahumma lā sahla illā mā jaʿaltahu sahlan wa anta tajʿal al-ḥazna idhā shiʾta sahlan* (Dear God, there is no easy path save that which You make easy, and whenever it is Your will You make rugged ground easy to tred)." From here it skips to "*qāla al-shaykh al-imām al-jāmiʿ bayna ʿilmay al-sharīʿah wa al-ḥaqīqah*" and continues in agreement with *I.Q.* up to "*āmīn,*" deleting the panegyric salutation upon the Prophet and his Companions. *N.K.* also refers to Ibn 'Aṭā' Allāh as "al-Iskandarī," instead of "al-Sakandarī."

1. O servant, seek from God at all times the inspiration and power to repent. Indeed, God* has invited you to this, saying, "*And repent to God, all of you, O Believers, perhaps you might succeed.*" [24:31] And He said, "*Verily God loves those who constantly repent, and He loves those who purify themselves.*" [2:222] And the Prophet* said, "Indeed, I repent to God seventy times a day."[2]

2. Now, if you want to achieve repentance, at no time during your life should you be devoid of reflection. Reflect upon what you have done during the day. If you find that you have been obedient to God, thank God for this. If you find that you have been disobedient, rebuke yourself, ask God for forgiveness, and turn to Him in repentance. Indeed, there is no audience with God more beneficial than one in which you are critical of yourself. But do not rebuke yourself in a state of laughter and merriment. Rather, rebuke yourself in a state of seriousness and honesty, openly scowling, with a heavy heart, crest-fallen and humiliated. If you do this, God will replace your sadness with happiness, your humiliation with dignity, the darkness that engulfs you with light, and the veil that obstructs your inner vision with disclosure.

3. On the authority of Shaykh Makīn al-Dīn al-Asmar (d. 692/1293)°,[3] who was one of the seven Pious Substitutes[4]: "Early in

2. See Abū ʿAbd Allāh Muḥammad b. Ismāʿīl al-Bukhārī, *Ṣaḥīḥ al-bukhārī* ed. Qāsim al-Shamāʿī al-Rifāʿī 9 vols. (Beirut: Dār al-Arqam b. Abī al-Arqam, N.d.), 8: 417, on the authority of Abū Hurayra: "I heard the Prophet say, 'By God, I ask God for forgiveness and repent to Him more than seventy times a day.'" See also Muslim b. Ḥajjāj, *Ṣaḥīḥ muslim*, 4 vols. (Beirut: Dār Ibn Ḥazm, 1416/1995), 4: 1648, on the authority of al-Agharr al-Muzanī: "Verily, my heart is assaulted (*yughān ʿalā*) and I ask God for forgiveness one hundred times a day." *J.K.*, 16; *N.K.* 12, gives the full text of the hadith on the authority of al-Agharr al-Muzanī in the body of the text.

3. Abū Muḥammad ʿAbd Allāh b. Manṣūr b. ʿAlī al-Lakhmī al-Iskandarānī. See Abū al-Falāḥ ʿAbd al-Ḥayy b. al-ʿImād al-Ḥanbalī, *Shadharāt al-dhabab fī tarīkh man dhahab*, 8 vols. (Beirut: Dār al-Āfāq al-Jadīdah, N.d.), 5: 421; Ṣalāḥ al-Dīn Khalīl b. Aybak al-Ṣafadī, *al-Wāfī bi al-wafayāt*, 17 vols., ed. D. Krawulsky (Weisbaden: Franz Steiner, 1982), 17: 643. According to both Ibn al-ʿImād and al-Ṣafadī, Makīn al-Dīn al-Asmar was "*shaykh al-qurrāʾ* (master of the Qurʾān reciters)" in Alexandria.

4. On "substitutes," see *E.I.*, "abdāl," 1: 94. While there is no universally agreed upon definition, the *abdāl*/s. *badal* are generally identified by a certain degree of spiritual accomplishment

my life, I used to sew for a living. I would mark my words during the day and at night call myself to account. I found that my words were few. Whenever I found good words, I praised God and thanked Him. When I found other than this, I repented to God and asked for His forgiveness." He continued to do this until he became a Pious Substitute, may God be pleased with him.

4. Know that if you have an agent who calls himself to account and holds himself responsible, you will have no need to do so, because he does it himself. But if he is remiss, you will call him to account and hold him responsible and even exaggerate in this regard. In a similar way,[5] all of your actions should pursue the interests of God.* And you should not think that you will do anything for which God will not call you to account and hold you responsible.

5. When a person commits a sin, this is accompanied by darkness. Indeed, disobedience is like fire, and darkness is its smoke. It is like someone kindling a fire in a room for seventy years. Do you not think that the roof of that room will be blackened? In the same way, the heart is blackened by disobedience. And nothing wipes it clean except repentance to God. Humiliation, darkness, and being veiled from God are thus natural accompaniments of disobedience. But when you repent to God, the effects of these sins disappear.

---

in the Sufi hierarchy of saints. *N.K.*, 14, nt. 1, reports that there are several hadith, e.g., in the *Musnad al-imām aḥmad* and *Majma' al-zawā'id* of al-Haythamī, in which the Prophet mentions *abdāl*, for example: "The Pious Substitutes of this Community are thirty in number, like the Intimate Friend of the All-Merciful (*khalīl al-raḥmān*); every time one of them dies, God substitutes another in his place." See also, however, Riḍā, *al-Manār*, 24: 514–515, where he cites Ibn Taymīya's calling all of these reports into question, and 27: 749–752, where Riḍā himself explicitly denounces all of these hadith as fabricated.

5. *N.K.*, 15 adds "*yā hādhā*" (good sir) here.

6. Neglect will find no way to you except through your own negligence in following the example of the Prophet*. And you will not be elevated in the sight of God except by following the example of the Prophet*.[6] Now, following his example takes two forms: outward and inward. The outward form is in such matters as prayer, fasting, alms, pilgrimage, jihad, and the like. The inward form is that your prayer be characterized by a connection with God and your recitation of Qur'ān by reflection upon Him. So when you perform an act of obedience such as prayer or recitation and find neither connection nor reflection, know that you are afflicted with some inner disease, be it arrogance, conceit, or some similar malady. Indeed, God* says, "*I will turn away from My signs those who unjustifiably proceed with arrogance in the land.*" [7: 146] In such instances, you will resemble a person who is wracked with fever in whose mouth sugar acquires a bitter taste. But (even in this context), disobedience in a state of humiliation and recognizing one's need for guidance is better than obedience in a state of vaingloriousness and arrogance.

7. God* said, relating the statement of Abraham, the Intimate Friend of God, upon him and upon our Prophet Muhammad be the best of salutations and most complete peace, "*Whoever follows me is from me.*" [14: 36] This implies that whoever does not follow him is not from him. God said, relating the statement of Noah, may the purest of salutations and peace be upon him and our Chosen Prophet,[7] "*Verily my son is from my family.*" [11: 45] To this God* replied, "*O Noah, he is not from your family. This is an unfit deed.*" [11: 46] Thus, the act of following someone renders the follower as if he were a part of the one followed, even if he is unrelated by blood, as was the case with Salmān al-Fārisī,° as indicated by the statement of

6. *N.K.*, 16: "*al-nabī al-mukarram wa al-rasūl al-mu'aẓẓam*" (the ennobled Prophet and venerated Messenger).

7. This panegyric is missing in *J.K.*, 20.

the Prophet*: "Salmān is a member of our household." It is well known, of course, that Salmān was a Persian. But because of his commitment to following the Prophet,[8] the Prophet made this noble statement about him,[9] in order to instruct us in this regard. And just as following someone establishes a bond of connectedness, its absence results in disconnectedness.

8. God has gathered the whole of goodness in a house and made its key following the example of the Prophet*.[10] So, follow him by being satisfied with what God has provided you, by eschewing and limiting your take of the pleasures of this world and by leaving that which does not concern you, of words as well as deeds.[11] And for whomever the door to following the example of the Prophet is opened, this will be an indication of God's love. Indeed, God* said, "*Say, (O Muhammad) if you love God then follow me; God will love you and forgive your sins. And God is forgiving, merciful.*" [3: 31]

9. So, if you want to seek the whole of goodness, say, "O Lord, I ask You the gift of following Your Messenger,[12] in his words and his deeds." And whoever desires this must abandon injustice to God's servants, regarding both their honor and their lineage. Indeed, were people to enjoy safety from each other's injustices, they would all hasten to God. But they are impeded from doing this, like a debtor whose movement is restricted by fear of debt-collectors.[13]

8. *N.K.*, 19 adds "*al-mukarram.*"
9. *N.K.*, 19 adds "*qāla 'anhu 'alayhi al-ṣalāt wa al-salām hādhā al-ḥadīth al-sharīf.*"
10. *N.K.*, 19, adds "*al-mukarram.*"
11. *N.K.*, 19 adds "*li qawlihi ṣalla Allāhu 'alayhi wa sallama min ḥusn islām al-mar' tarkuhu mā lā ya'nīh* (based on his statement, God's blessings and salutations be upon him, 'It is a sign of the health of a person's Islam that they avoid that which does not concern them.')."
12. *N.K.*, 20 adds "*wa ḥabībika wa rasūlika wa ṣafīyika wa najīyika Muḥammad* (Your beloved, Your messenger, Your sincere friend, Your confidant Muhammad)."
13. This is perhaps a premodern take on the modern aversion to "organized religion." Through their misdeeds, injustices, and vile misrepresentations, as well as their support for or acquiescence in the face of blatantly oppressive, unempathetic and discriminatory socio-political or economic orders, all in ways that violate scripture, those who set themselves

10. Know that were you taken into the favor of a king and granted intimate access to him and then someone to whom you owed money came petitioning you for it, you would be annoyed, even if the amount were trifling. How, then, do you imagine yourself when you come on the Day of Judgment and one hundred thousand or more persons come seeking redress for various trespasses that you have committed against them in the way of taking their money, impugning their honor, or other such wrongs? What will be your state?

11. The truly afflicted is he whose sins and carnal passions ravage him to the point of rendering him as a tattered water-skin.[14] This is the pathetic wretch whose food and carnal desires amount to little more than filling his toilet and pleasing his spouse. And would that all of this had been lawfully procured and executed!

12. Thus, the first station is repentance. And nothing that is done subsequently is accepted in the absence of repentance.

13. A person who engages in sinful behavior is like a brand new pot beneath which a flame is lit for a duration, as a result of which its bottom blackens. If you hasten to wash it, this blackness will be washed away. But if you leave it and cook in it time and again, this blackness will settle into it to the point that it crusts and washing it will be of no use. Repentance is what washes away the soot of the heart, such that deeds emerge carrying the scent of being accepted by God. So constantly ask God* for repentance. And if you attain

---

up as representatives of religion often turn people away from God and prevent them from turning to Him. See also below on charlatans, ¶ 270.

14. *I.Q.*, 14; *Shaqrūn*, 5; *N.K.*, 21: *ka al-shann al-bālī*; *J.K.*, 24: *ka al-shay' al-bālī*. The image here is of one whose outward appearance conceals his or her inner emptiness and lack of sustained focus and true commitment, like a water-skin that has a barely perceptible hole in it, as a result of which all of its water escapes over time without its owner knowing it. Then, when the owner finds himself or herself in need of water, there is none there to sustain them. Similarly, the habitually inwardly sinful but outwardly religious person's religion is lost over time without his or her knowing it.

this, your time will be well spent. For this is a gift from God that He places in whomever He pleases among His servants. A tattered, humble servant may attain it while his master does not; a woman may attain it while her husband does not; a young person may attain it, while one advanced in years does not. So if you attain it, (know that) God has made you the object of His love, in accordance with His statement, "*Verily God loves those who constantly repent and He loves those who purify themselves.*" [2: 222]

14. But only one who knows the value of a thing[15] is made happy by it. Thus, were you to cast an emerald among a flock of beasts, barley would be more preferable to them. So observe: to which group do you belong? If you repent, you are among the loved. If you do not, you are among the wrongdoers. God* says, "*And whoever does not repent, they are among the wrong-doers.*" [49: 11]

15. Whoever repents wins; whoever does not loses. And do not despair, saying, "How often I repent only to contradict my repentance." For the sick person hopes for life as long as his spirit remains in him.

16. When a person repents, his house in paradise, the heavens, the earth, and (even) the Prophet* rejoice for him. Indeed, God* is not pleased by your state of loving Him but rather by your state of being loved by Him. And how can one who is loved be compared to one who simply loves?[16]

17. Fie on the one who knows the goodness of the Benefactor yet has the gall to disobey Him. Then again, one who prefers to disobey Him does not really know His goodness. One who is not

15. *I.Q.*, 15; *Shaqrūn*, 6; *J.K.*, 26: *innamā yaghtabiṭ bi al-shay' man ya'rif qadrah*; *N.K.*, 22: *innamā yatta'iẓ bi al-shay' man ya'rif qadrah* (But only one who knows the value of a thing will heed the lessons to be learned from it).

16. Recall here his citation of the verse, "*Verily God loves those who constantly repent and He loves those who purify themselves*" (2: 222) in ¶ 13.

mindful of Him does not know His power. And one who busies himself with other than Him will not prosper. Such a person knows that the self beckons to destruction but follows it anyway. He knows that the heart[17] beckons to guidance but disobeys it all the same. He knows the stature of the One he disobeys but flaunts disobedience before Him nonetheless. If such a person knew the magnitude of His grandeur, he would not openly defy Him. But he knows how close His Lord is to him and that He sees him; yet he rushes to do what He forbids. He knows the effects of sin, in this world and the next, secretly and manifestly; yet he shows no shame before his Lord.[18] If such a person knew that he was in His grip, he would not openly violate His commandments.

18. Know that sin entails the breaking of the covenant, the undoing of the bond of love, and preferring something else over the Master; it entails submission to undisciplined passion, casting off the robe of modesty, and defiantly confronting God with that with which He is not pleased. This is not to mention its outward effects on the sinner, such as the appearance of weariness in the limbs, paleness in the eyes, lethargy in tendering service, loss of respect for the sacred, bearing the aura of being consumed[19] by carnal desire, and the loss of satisfaction with acts of obedience.

19. As for the inward effects, these include hardening of the heart, intransigence of the self, cramping of the breast with carnal desires, losing the sweetness that normally accompanies obedience, being inundated by distractions that short-circuit flashes of illumination, and the coming to power of the empire of undisciplined passion. This is in addition to the swelling of doubt and obliviousness to one's ultimate end and the depths of reckoning (that await).

17. Heart, or "*qalb*," here is a metaphor for conscience.

18. *J.K.*, 28 casts this and the preceding sentence as conditionals, using the subjunctive "*law*."

19. *I.Q.*, 16; *N.K.*, 26: *kasb al-shahawāt*; *Shaqrūn*, 7: *kasb al-shahwah*; *J.K.*, 29, *kashf al-shahawāt*.

20. Were there nothing in disobedience but a change of name, this would suffice. When you are obedient, you are called an energetic promoter of good; but when you are disobedient, you are called a recalcitrant promoter of evil. This is the matter regarding the change of name. How much more will be the change in effect, from the sweetness of obedience to the sweetness of disobedience, from the deliciousness of servitude to God to the deliciousness of (servitude to) carnal desire? This is the matter regarding the change in effect. How much more will be the change of description? After you had been described before God as a person of good qualities, the matter is reversed and you are described as a person of evil states. This is the matter regarding the change in description. How much more will be the change of rank? After you had been among the righteous before God, you become one of the corrupt. And after you had been among the God-conscious, you become one of the traitors.

21. If sin is openly manifested before you, seek God's help and repair to Him. Throw dirt on your head and say, "O God, take me from the humility of disobedience to the honor of obedience." Visit the graves of the saints and the righteous and say in supplication, "O Most Merciful of the Merciful."

22. Is it your aim to engage your self in battle while you strengthen it by catering to its carnal desires to the point that they overtake you? Are you not ignorant? The heart is a tree that is irrigated with the water of obedience. Its fruit is its emotional states. The fruit of the eye is careful observation. The fruit of the ear is listening to the Qur'ān. The fruit of the tongue is remembrance of God. And the fruit of the hands and feet is going forth in pursuit of good. But when the heart dries up, these fruits all fall. So whenever drought sets in, increase your supplications in remembrance of God. And do not be like the sick person who says, "I will not

treat my illness until I find the definitive cure." For it will be said to you, "You will not find the definitive cure until you commit to treating your illness." There is no sweetness in jihad; there is but the jagged edges of swords. So prosecute the jihad against your self. That is the greatest jihad.

23. Know that the bereaved mother has no cause for celebration. Celebration is simply for the one who overpowers his self. There is no celebration except for one who properly marshals his powers. One of them passed by a monk's convent and asked, "O monk, when is these people's day of celebration?" He replied, "The day that God forgives them."[20]

24. In dealing with your self, you are no different from a man who finds his wife in a wine-seller's tavern and then brings her seductive clothing and sensuous dishes. And when she fails to perform the prayer, he feeds her brayed wheat and all kinds of delectable delights.[21]

25. One of them went forty years without attending a single religious gathering because of the putridness of the hearts of the heedless attendees he used to smell.[22] How knowledgeable you are concerning the interests of this world! But how ignorant you are concerning the interests of your Afterlife!

26. Living in this world, you are like an individual who goes out to a pasture and works hard and stores up staples. You gather that which benefits you here and now.[23] But when you store up snakes of carnal desire and scorpions of disobedience, you

20. *I.Q.*, 18: *yawma yaghfiru Allāh lahum*; *J.K.*, 33; *Shaqrūn*, 8, *N.K.*, 30: *yawma yughfaru lahum*.
21. *I.Q.*, 18: *aṣbaḥa yuṭʿimuhā*; *Shaqrūn*, 8; *N.K.*, 31: *aṣbaḥta tuṭʿimuhā*; *J.K.*, 33, *aṣbaḥta tulqimuhā*.
22. *N.K.*, 32 adds here "*yā hādhā*" (Good sir).
23. *I.Q.*, 19, *J.K.*, 33 adds *fī waqtih* (at that immediate time).

destroy yourself.[24] How ignorant you are! People store up staples for their time of need, while you merely store up that which harms you, namely acts of disobedience! Do you see anyone who brings poisonous snakes into their home and raises them? This is what you do.

27. The most harmful thing to be feared for you are those lesser sins that you trivialize. For you may appreciate the gravity of major sins and thus repent of them. But you trivialize the minor sins and thus do not repent of them. Your likeness here is that of a person who happens upon a lion from which God saves him. Then he comes upon fifty wolves that overtake him. God said, "*You take it to be negligible, while it is in the sight of God grave indeed.*" [24: 15][25] Major sins (in and of themselves) may be (rendered) negligible by the grace of God. But when you persist in committing a minor sin, it becomes major. For poison, even in small amounts, can kill. The minor sin is like a spark of fire. And a single spark can burn down an entire city.

28. Whoever fritters away his health and well-being on disobedience to God is like a person whose father leaves him an inheritance of a thousand gold *dīnār*s and he goes and spends it on poisonous snakes and scorpions with which he proceeds to surround himself. Now bitten by this one, now stung by that one, will they not eventually kill him?

24. *Shaqrūn*, 8: *fa qad atayta bimā ya'ūdu naf'uhu 'alayka fī waqtihi wa anta khazanta ḥayyāti al-shahawāt*; *I.Q.*, 19: *fa anta qad atayta bimā ya'ūdu naf'uhu 'alayka fī waqtihi wa in khazanta ḥayyāti al-shahawāt*; *J.K.*, 34: *fa anta mā atayta bimā ya'ūdu naf'uhu 'alayka fī waqtihi bal khazanta al-shahawāt wa mā taḥyā bihi al-shahawāt*; *N.K.*, 32: *fa qad atayta bimā ya'ūdu naf'uhu 'alayka fa ḥaraqtahu* (which you simply burn up).

25. *N.K.*, 33 alone adds here *wa qāla rasūl Allāh, ṣalla Allāhu 'alayhi wa sallama lā ṣaghīrata ma'a al-iṣrār wa lā kabīrata ma'a al-istighfār* (The Prophet* said, "There is no minor sin where there is persistence, and there is no major sin where there is a plea for forgiveness").

29. You waste away hours violating His will. You are like a buzzard who hovers in search of dead corpses; wherever it finds one, it descends upon it. Instead[26] be like a bee, small in size but great in ambition; it gathers good and brings forth good.

30. For as long as you have wallowed in places of tribulation, wallow now in God's affections. This is the reality that will show you the way. But alas, one who is deadened by heedlessness will not be discouraged by setbacks. Indeed, the dim-witted woman laughs at the death of her own child. In the same way, you turn away from night vigils and days of fasting and none of your limbs feel any pain.[27] And the only reason for this is that heedlessness has deadened your heart. For the live person is pained by the prick of a needle, while the dead person feels no pain even if he should be cut to pieces with swords. You are afflicted with a dead heart.[28] Thus, attend the sessions of wisdom; for in them are wafts of Paradise. You will find them on your way there, in your home and in your quarters. So do not miss a session, even if you are in a state of sinfulness. And do not say, "What benefit shall I derive from attending such sessions while I remain steeped in sin[29] and am unable to leave it?" The archer must continue to shoot! If he does not take home game today, he will take it tomorrow.

31. Know this, good sir: Disobedience may be a cause of your provisions' discontinuance;[30] so beware of disobedience. Ask God for repentance. If your petition is accepted, all well and good. If not, ask for God's help. "*Our Lord, we have wronged ourselves, and if You do*

26. *J.K.*, 36 alone has *bal* (Nay) here.

27. I have ignored the "*wa*" before "*lā tata'allam*" in *I.Q.*, *J.K.*, and *N.K* and "*lam tata'allam*" in *Shaqrūn*.

28. *N.K.*, 35 has *fa anta ḥayy bi al-jasad mayyit bi al-qalb* (You have a live body but a dead heart).

29. *I.Q.*, 20; *Shaqrūn*, 10; *J.K.* 37: *wa anā a'ṣī*; *N.K.*, 35: *wa anā a'ṣī rabbī*.

30. *I.Q.*, 21; *Shaqrūn*, 10; *J.K.*, 38: *li tawaqquf al-rizq*; *N.K.*, 36: *li tawqīf al-rizq*.

not forgive us and have mercy on us, we will be among the losers." [7:23] And do not be like one who comes upon forty years of life and has never petitioned at God's door.

32. The thing most dreaded for you is a bad end[31]—may God save us from that—due to the amber of faith being extinguished by the blackness[32] of disobedience, i.e., sin upon sin with no repentance to the point that the heart is blackened.

33. Beware[33] of lackadaisicalness in your (morally relevant) deeds, while you are meticulous in choosing those delightful indulgences that simply fill your toilet. And beware of the self that is between your two loins;[34] for it accretes things against you,[35] refusing to leave you until death. Even Satan, on the other hand, leaves you during the month of Ramadan, when devils are chained up.[36] And you may find that people murder and steal during this month. This, however, is from the self. So whenever it inclines toward disobedience, remind it of God's punishment and the disconnectedness from God that results therefrom. Indeed, poisoned honey is abandoned, despite one's knowledge of its sweetness, because of the harm it carries.

34. As the Prophet* said, "The life of this world is sweet and lush,"[37] and in another narration, "a putrid corpse."[38] It is sweet and

31. *I.Q.*, 21; *Shaqrūn*, 10; *J.K.*, 38: *sū' al-khātimah*; *N.K.*, 36: *min sū' al-khātimah*.
32. *I.Q.*, 21; *Shaqrūn*, 10: *sawād al-'iṣyān*; *J.K.*, 38, *N.K.*, 36: *sū' al-'iṣyān*.
33. *N.K.*, 37 *has iyyāka thumma iyyāka* (Beware, I say, beware).
34. *I.Q.*, 21; *Shaqrūn* 10; *J.K.*, 39: *wa'ḥdhar nafsaka allatī bayna janbayk*; *N.K.*, 37: *wa'ḥdhar kulla al-ḥidhr min nafsika fa inna a'dā 'adūwayka nafsuka allatī bayna janbayk* (And take the greatest precautions with your self; for the deadliest of your two enemies is your self which is between your two loins).
35. *I.Q.*, 21; *Shaqrūn*, 10; *N.K.*, 37: *taḥṭab 'alayka*: *J.K.*, 39: *taghlib 'alayka*.
36. See *Ṣaḥīḥ muslim*, 2: 622.
37. In *Ṣaḥīḥ muslim*, 4: 1667–68, there is a hadith that states verbatim, "The life of this world is sweet and lush . . ." and warns against being seduced by its seductive powers. There is no alternative narration, however, that describes it as a "putrid corpse."
38. *J.K.*, 39 has "*jīfah qadhirah 'ind marā'ī al-nufūs*" before "*jīfah qadhirah 'ind marā'ī al-qulūb*, which appears neither in *I.Q.*, 22, *Shaqrūn*, 10 or *N.K.*, 38. Meanwhile, the editor of *J.K.*,

lush to the people of heedlessness, a putrid corpse to the intelligent, sweet and lush to the self, a putrid corpse before the mirrors of the heart, sweet and lush as a means of admonishing, a putrid corpse as a means of repelling. So do not be in the least bit fooled by its sweetness. For its ultimate end is bitter.

35. If you are asked, "Who is a believer?" Say, "One who is aware of his own faults and does not attribute faults to others." [39]And if you are asked, "Who is abandoned?" Say, "One who attributes faults to others while absolving himself of any and all."

36. Among the things to which the people of our time have habituated themselves is consorting and fraternizing with the disobedient. And had they frowned in the latter's faces that would have discouraged them from being disobedient.[40]

37. Were He to open for you the door to perfection, you would not return to vile deeds. Can you imagine one for whom the doors of palaces are opened; would they return to garbage heaps?[41] Were He to open for you the door of intimacy between you and Him, you would not seek intimacy with anyone else. Were He to choose you to witness His lordship, He would not sever your connection to Him. Were you to show Him high-mindedness, He would not consign you to any other.

---

39 nt. 2 states that he has not been able to locate the "putrid corpse" version of this hadith in any of the nine collections he consulted. At *I.Q.*, 22 nt. 3, the editors trace a similar statement to ʿAlī b. Abī Ṭālib, recorded by al-Hindī in *Kanz al-ʿummāl*. *N.K.*, 38, nt. 2 makes a similar attribution to ʿAlī b. Abī Ṭālib.

39. *N.K.*, 39 adds, *li qawl al-nabī ṣallā Allāhu ʿalayhi wa sallama wa idhā aḥabba Allahu ʿabdan baṣṣarahu bi ʿuyūb nafsih* (In accordance with the statement of the Prophet*, "When God loves a person, He grants them insight into their own flaws.").

40. *I.Q.*, 23; *Shaqrūn* 11; *J.K.*, 40: *la kāna dhālika zājiran lahum ʿan al-maʿṣiyah*; *N.K.*, 40, *la kāna dhālika khayran lahum wa zajran lahum ʿan al-maʿṣiyah* (that would have been better for them and a means of discouraging them from disobedience).

41. *I.Q.*, 23; *Shaqrūn*, 11; *J.K.*, 41: *law fataḥa laka bāb al-kamāl lamā rajaʿta ilā al-radhāʾil* . . . ; *N.K.*, 40 deletes this entire segment and begins with, *law fataḥa laka bāb al-uns*. . . . (Were He to open for you the door of intimacy between you and Him. . . .).

And should He remove from you the love you have for any created being, you should rejoice; for this is a function of His caring for you.[42]

38. Disobedience is invariably accompanied by humiliation. Shall you disobey Him, while He honors you? On the contrary, He has tied honor to obedience and humiliation to disobedience. Thus, obeying Him becomes light, honor, and a lifting of the veil, while its opposite is disobedience, darkness, humiliation, and a veil between you and Him.[43] And you are only prevented from witnessing (this reality) by your failure to observe the proper limits and by your preoccupation with this earthly existence.

39. If your child disobeys, discipline him according to the religious law. But do not cut him off. Rather, frown at him, so that he desists from disobedience. When the believer disobeys, the thing that most frequently comes over him is disquieting anxiety,[44] i.e., that his friends[45] will either scandalize or ridicule him. But alas, when they do that, they too go astray.

40. When a believer disobeys, he falls into a great dilemma.[46] But the way to deal with him is to do what you do in the case of your child when he disobeys: you turn away from him outwardly while inwardly making him the object of pity, secretly praying for him to be restored.

42. Perspicaciously, if counterintuitively, Ibn 'Aṭā' Allāh appears to recognize both the limits and dual character of love, as an emotion capable of producing much evil, even as it is capable of producing great good.

43. *I.Q.*, 23, *N.K.*, 40–41: *fa ṣārat ṭā'atuhu nūran wa 'izzan wa kashfa ḥijābin wa ḍidduhā ma'ṣīyatun wa ẓulmatun wa dhullun . . .* ; *Shaqrūn*, 11: *fa ṣārat fī ṭā'atihi nūrun wa 'izzun wa kashfu ḥijābin wa ḍidduhā ma'ṣīyatun ẓulmatun wa dhullun . . .* ; *J.K.*, 42: *fa ṣārat ṭā'atuhu nūran wa 'izzan wa kashfa ḥijābin wa ḍidduhā al-ma'ṣīyatu ẓulmatun wa dhullun wa ḥijābun.*

44. *I.Q.*, 24; *Shaqrūn*, 11: *al-dakhal*; *J.K.*, 42: *al-khajal* (embarrassment); *N.K.*, 41: al-*dakhīl* (a snooper).

45. *J.K.*, 42 has *rufaqā'uh*, which appears in neither *I.Q.*, 24, *Shaqrūn*, 11, nor *N.K.*, 41.

46. *I.Q.*, 24; *Shaqrūn*11: *warṭah*; *J.K.*, 42 *waḥlah* (*warṭah*); *N.K.*, 41: *wahlah* (terror).

41. It is ignorant enough of you that you should envy people of worldly means and allow your heart to become preoccupied with what they have. This makes you more ignorant than them. For, while they are preoccupied with what they have been given, you are preoccupied with what you have not.

42. Your eyes become inflamed and you rush to treat them. And the only reason for this is that through them you have been able to behold the delights of this world. Thus you rush to treat them so that none of these worldly pleasantries escape your vision. But your inner vision remains afflicted with disease for forty years, and you do nothing to treat it.

43. Know that a life the early years of which have been wasted deserves to have its latter years preserved, like a woman who has ten children nine of whom die and one of whom remains. Will not her affections redound[47] upon that remaining child? You have wasted most of your life. So preserve the rest; for it is but a few dregs in an otherwise empty glass. By God, your life does not begin the day you were born; it begins the day you come to know God*.

44. What a difference there is between the people of felicity and the people of misery. When people of felicity see a person engaged in disobedience to God they outwardly rebuke him while inwardly praying for him. People of misery, on the other hand, rebuke him publicly in pursuit of self-gratification, and they may even impugn his character.[48] The believer is one who is sincere to his fellows in private and seeks to cover their faults in public. People of misery, however, are the opposite: when they see a person engaged in disobedience, they slam the door of repentance in his face and

47. *I.Q.*, 25; *Shaqrūn*, 12; *J.K.*, 45: *taruddu wujduhā*; *N.K.*, 43: *taruddu waḥdahā*.
48. *I.Q.*, 25: *thalabū*; *Shaqrūn*, 12; *J.K.*, 46; *N.K.*, 44: *thalamū*.

scandalize him. Such people's inner vision is unlit, and they are far removed from God.

45. If you want to gauge a man's intellect, observe him when you mention others to him. If you find him indulging[49] every evil construction to the point that he says, "Forget so and so; he has committed such and such evil deeds," know that his inner being is desolate and that he is devoid of knowledge. But if you see that he mentions people favorably or that he refers to their condemnable acts by putting favorable constructions on them, saying things like, "Maybe they had a lapse[50] or a valid excuse," and similar exculpations, know that his inner being is filled with life. For the believer proceeds on the assumption that his fellow Muslims are honorable people.

46. Whoever approaches the end of life and wants to make up for what he has missed, let him busy himself with comprehensive supplications. For if he does this, his short life will become long in effect. For example, he might say, "Glory be to God Almighty, and may He be praised, as plentifully as the number of His creatures, in proportions that please His self, on a magnitude as great as His Throne, and as expansively as the scope of His words."[51] Likewise, one who has failed to engage in much fasting and night vigils should preoccupy himself with sending blessings upon the Prophet*. For should you fulfill God's every commandment throughout your life then God should send a single blessing upon you, this single blessing would outweigh all of the acts of obedience that you have performed throughout your entire life. This is because you send blessings upon the Prophet in proportion to your capacity, while He sends blessings

49. *I.Q.*, 26; *Shaqrūn*, 12: *fa in wajadtahu yaṭūfu 'alā maḥmal sū'*; *J.K.*, 46: *fa in wajadtahu malhūfan 'alā maḥmal sū'*.

50. *I.Q.*, 26; *Shaqrūn*, 13; *J.K.*, 46; *la'allahu sahā*; *N.K.*, 45: *la'allahu yantahī*.

51. See *Ṣaḥīḥ muslim*, 4: 1660.

upon you in proportion to His lordship. This is the case if He sends a single blessing. So what if, as indicated in the sound hadith, He was to send ten blessings upon you every time you send a single blessing upon the Prophet?[52] How beautiful a life is when lived in obedience to God through remembrance of God* or sending blessings upon the Prophet*!

47. It is related that game-animals are only captured and trees only cut down because of their intermittent lapses in the remembrance of God*. No burglar burglarizes a house while its inhabitants are awake. Rather, he does so during their lapses or when they are asleep.

48. Anyone who knows that his time of departure[53] is near hastens to prepare for it. Anyone who knows that the good deeds of others will not benefit him strives earnestly to do good himself. Anyone who is retired without taking account of their life suffers loss without knowing it. And anyone who appoints an agent and discovers his treachery will fire him. This is the case with your self: you have discovered its treachery, so remove it from authority and restrict its means of access.

49. If you see willful neglect,[54] unbridled carnal desire, and heedlessness in yourself, this is your natural profile. But if you see penitence, godly fear, and abstinence, this is the handiwork of God. It is like seeing alfa, figs, and boxthorn where you live, as these plants are native to your land. But if you see peony, ripe dates, musk, and ambergris, know that this has been brought to

52. *N.K.*, 47 has *bi kulli ṣalāh tuṣallīhā ʿalā ḥabībihi muḥammad ṣalla Allāh ʿalayhi wa sallama.* As for this hadith itself, it is related that the Prophet* said, "Whoever sends a single blessing upon me, God will send ten blessings upon them and wipe out ten of their bad deeds." See *Musnad al-imām aḥmad,* 3: 102.

53. *N.K.*, adds *min al-bilād* (from a country).

54. *N.K.*, 48 adds *min ṭāʿat Allāh* (of obedience to God).

you via the handiwork of God. For these things are not native to your land. Musk is from Iraqi gazelles, and ambergris is from the Indian Ocean.

50. The likeness of you and your faith when you disobey God* is that of the sun during a solar eclipse or a lamp over which a sheet of paper is placed: it is there, but that which covers it blocks its light. In such circumstances, you should attend the gatherings at the mosque to restore your faculties. Even if your life is short, it will become long in effect through the attainment of faith, humility, self-effacement, godly fear, contemplation, remembrance, and the like. Had you known true faith, you would not have approached disobedience. But alas, there is no debtor more delinquent than the self, no enemy greater than Satan, and no opponent stronger than undisciplined passion.

51. Nothing repels provisions descending from God as does arrogance. For rain only settles on the plains, not on mountaintops. This is the likeness of the hearts of the arrogant. Mercy rolls off of them and falls upon the hearts of the humble. And by arrogant we mean those who reject the truth, not those who have fine clothing. Indeed, arrogance is disregard for the truth, i.e., pushing it aside, and contempt for people. And do not think that arrogance only resides in people of power or wealth. On the contrary, it may reside in one who does not have enough food for a single night. Yet he spreads corruption instead of good, due to his arrogance toward God's creatures.[55]

52. Do not think that the wretched one is one who is a prisoner of war or is incarcerated. The wretched one is one who disobeys God and brings into this pure kingdom the impurity of disobedience.

55. *Shaqrūn*, 14; *J.K.*, 50, *N.K.*, 51: *li annahu takabbara ʿalā khalq Allāh taʿālā*; *I.Q.*, 29: *li annahu takabbara ʿalā ḥaqq Allāh taʿālā*.

53. There are many who invest *dīnār*s and *dirhams*. But those who invest their spirit are few.[56]

54. The idiot is one who takes to crying upon the death of his child but cries not over what he has lost with God*. It is as if he says by his actions, "I am crying over that which used to distract me from my Lord." But he should have rejoiced at this loss and repaired to his Lord for having taken from him that which used to distract him from Him.

55. It is foul of you[57] that your hair should turn gray while you remain juvenile and childish in your intellect, not understanding what God wants of you. If you are intelligent, cry over yourself before you are cried over. For your children, your wife, your servants, and your friends do not (really) cry over you when you die. They simply cry over what they no longer enjoy of you. So precede them in this regard, and say, "It is fitting that I should cry over what I have forfeited of my fortune from my Lord before you[58] all cry over me."

56. It is ignorant enough of you that your Lord treats you in a manner that bespeaks trustworthiness, while you treat Him in a manner that bespeaks contempt.

57. A true man is not simply one who is able to raise his voice among people at gatherings. A true man is one who is able to raise his voice against his self and turn it back toward God*.

58. Whoever is weighed down by the concerns of this world and abandons concern for the Afterlife is like a person who is fleeing from a lion seeking to make him his prey but is then bitten by a flea,

56. *N.K.*, 51, *J.K.*, 51: *kathīr man anfaqa al-danānīr wa al-darāhim wa lākin man anfaqa al-rūḥ qalīl; Shaqrūn*, 14: *kathīr man anfaqa al-danānīr wa al-darāhim wa lākin min al-rūḥ qalīl; I. Q.*, 30: *kathīr man anfaqa al-danānīr wa al-darāhim wa lākin man anfaqa al-dam*ʿ *(tears) qalīl.*

57. *N.K.*, 52 adds *yā hādhā* (good sir).

58. *N.K.*, 52 has *qabla an yabkūn* [*sic*] (before they cry).

at which time his attention is diverted away from the lion. Whoever is heedless of God busies himself with trifles. And whoever is not heedless of Him only busies himself with Him. Thus, the best state you can be in is one in which you forfeit the vanities of this life in order to attain the Afterlife. But how often the Afterlife escapes you in your pursuit of the vanities of this world!

59. How disgraceful cowardice is in the soldier; how disgraceful solecisms are in the grammarian; and how disgraceful it is of one who feigns asceticism in order to pursue the vanities of this world!

60. The true man is not the one who trains you by his statements. The true man is one who trains you by your simply observing him. On the authority of Shaykh Abū al-ʿAbbās al-Mursī (d. 686/1287)°: "If turtles rear their offspring by simple observation, so should the master rear his disciples. Turtles lay their eggs on land, then take to the banks of rivers and look back at their eggs. God then rears their young for them by means of their simply looking at them."

61. Do not dare leave this abode without tasting the sweetness of His love. And the sweetness of His love is not in food or drink; for unbelievers and dumb beasts share in this. Rather, join the angels in tasting the sweetness[59] of remembrance and unadulterated concentration on God. For (pure) spirits cannot withstand the (impure) splashes[60] from the self. Indeed, when you immerse yourself in the dead swamp of this world you become unfit for communion. For, those who are stained by the impurities of disobedience cannot come into the presence of God. Cleanse your heart of defects, the door to the unseen will open for you. Repent to God[61] and turn to Him in penitence and remembrance, the door will open for

59. *N.K.*, 55: *ḥālat al-dhikr* (the state of remembrance).

60. *I.Q.*, 32, *Shaqrūn*, 16; *J.K.*, 54: *rashāsh al-nufūs*; *N.K.*, 55: *wasāwis al-nufūs* (the whisperings of the self).

61. *N.K.*, 55 adds here *wa adim al-fikr* (and continue to reflect).

whomever continues to knock. In fact, were it not for a sense of decorum, we would not state the matter this way. For in reality, it is as Rābi'ah al-'Adawīyah° (185/801) said: "When was the door ever shut such that it would have to be opened?"[62]

62. What we mention here, however, is simply an entrance via which you can gain closeness to Him. But beware of your heart's falling into obliviousness of the oneness of God*. For the first stages of those who remember God is their calling to mind His* oneness. And it is only by such recollections that rememberers are able to remember Him and are granted spiritual insights. And they are only cast out of His presence by acts of remembrance that are shot through with obliviousness. You must seek assistance against this through subduing the two repositories of carnal desire: the stomach and the private parts. And it is only your self that will oppose you in your relationship with God.

63. How frequent your attempts are to gain favor with the people. How seldom your attempts are to gain favor with God!

64. Were the door to gaining favor with God opened for you, you would see wonders. Two units of prayer in the dead of night is a means of gaining favor; visiting the sick is a means of gaining favor; attending funeral prayers is a means of gaining favor; charity to the poor is a means of gaining favor; helping your fellow Muslim is a means of gaining favor; removing nuisances from public thoroughfares is a means of gaining favor. But alas, the discarded sword cries out for a willing arm.

62. In contradistinction to *I.Q.*, 32, *Shaqrūn*, 16, and *N.K.*, 55, *J.K.*, 55 has *kamā qālat al-sayyidah rābi'ah taqūl fī al-yawm 'asā wa fī ghadin minhu la'alla man qara'a al-bāb dakhala wa matā ughliqa hādhā al-bāb ḥattā yuftaḥ* (You say to yourself, "Maybe today," then the day after that you say, "Perhaps today." Whoever knocks on the door will ultimately enter. Indeed, when was this door ever closed such that it would have to be opened?).

65. There is no act of worship more beneficial to you than remembrance of God. For the elderly and the sick who are incapable of standing, bending, or prostrating are able to do this.

66. Know that the scholars and sages give you knowledge of how to gain access to God*. Do you imagine that when a slave is first purchased he is prepared to enter into service? On the contrary, he is assigned to someone who will train him and teach him proper etiquette. If he responds positively and learns this, he will be presented to the king. This is the likeness of the saints°. Their disciples accompany them for a time after which they thrust[63] their disciples into the divine presence. This is what people in general do when they want to teach a child how to swim: they go along with him by his side to the point that he is able to swim alone. When he becomes proficient, they thrust him into the depths and leave him on his own.

67. Beware of believing that you cannot benefit[64] from prophets, saints, and righteous people. For God has made them a means to Himself. Indeed, every miracle the saints perform—defying the laws of nature, walking on water, flying through the air, reporting on the unseen, springing water (from their fingers), and such—is a testimony to the truth of the Prophet*. For they have only been granted the ability to do these things because of their association with the prophets.[65]

68. On the authority of Shaykh Abū al-Ḥasan al-Shādhilī (d. 656/1258)°: "Measure and weigh yourself by prayer. If it engenders a sense of satisfaction, know that you are fortunate. God* says, '*Verily*

63. *N.K.*, 59: *yataraqqaw bihim* (they elevate their disciples).

64. *I.Q.*, 34; *J.K.*, 57: *iyyāka an ta'taqid annahu lā yuntafa' bi al-anbiyā'*; *Shaqrūn*, 17, *N.K.*, 59: *iyyāka an ta'taqid annahu lā yutawassal bi al-anbiyā'*. *I.Q.*, 34 nt. 1 states explicitly, however, that their manuscript reads "*yuntafa'*."

65. *J.K.*, 58 adds *wa li ḥusn mutāba'atihim*, in contradistinction to *I.Q.*, *Shaqrūn*, and *N.K.*

prayer preempts lewdness and vice.' [29:45][66] Otherwise, cry for yourself, as you literally drag your feet to prayer. Can you imagine a lover who does not wish to meet his beloved?[67] Thus, whoever wants to know the reality of their relationship with God and wants to examine their state with God, let him look at his prayer. It will either be performed with tranquility and humility or with heedlessness and haste. If it is not the former, then throw dirt on your head.[68] For one who sits in the presence of a musk-merchant will invariably pick up and carry something of his scent. And prayer is sitting in the presence of God*. So when you sit in His company and neither pick up nor carry anything from Him, this points to a disease in your heart, be it arrogance, conceit, or a simple lack of etiquette. God says, '*I will turn away from My signs those who unjustifiably proceed with arrogance in the land.'* [7: 146] Thus, one should not hasten to exit from prayer.[69] Rather, one should remain and remember God* and ask for forgiveness for all of the shortcomings in one's prayer. For many a prayer is there that is not fit for acceptance. But if you follow it by asking God for forgiveness, it will be accepted. (Even) the Prophet* used to follow his prayer by asking God for forgiveness three times."

69. How many latent deficiencies lie within you! When they are come upon by the vicissitudes of life, you manifest them openly. The most sinful of these is entertaining doubt about God. And having doubt about your provisions is to have doubt about The Provider.

70. The vanities of this world should be too trifling to weigh you down. But spiritual ambition has dwindled, such that the small minded are weighed down. Were you a person of greatness, you

66. *N.K.*, 60 omits this verse here.
67. *N.K.*, 60 adds the verse here and cites it to its end.
68. *I.Q.*, 35; *N.K.*, 61: *fa'ḥthu al-turāb 'alā ra'sik*; *Shaqrūn*, 17: *fa'ḥthu ra'saka*; *J.K.*, 59: *fa'ḥthu al-turāb 'alā wajhika wa ra'sik.*
69. *N.K.*, 61 has *al-khurūj min al-masjid* (to exit from the mosque).

would be concerned about great things. And anyone who is weighed down by minor concerns while ignoring major concerns, we deem to be of little intelligence.

71. Fulfill your commitments in the form of your duties of servitude, He will fulfill His commitments to you. Shall He provide for the dung beetle, the gecko,[70] and cockroaches but forget to provide for you? God* says, "*Command your family to pray and be steadfast in doing so. We do not ask you for provisions. It is We who provide for you. And the ultimate outcome favors God-consciousness.*" [20: 132]

72. For everyone who observes God's* right upon them, God will not introduce into His kingdom anything without informing them thereof. One of them looked upon a group and said to them, "Is there anyone among you whom God* informs whenever He introduces anything into His kingdom?" They responded, "No." He said, "Weep for yourselves."

73. The Pious Ancestors of old° used to ask a person about how they were doing in order to elicit their expressions of thanks to God. Today, however, people should not ask others how they are doing. For if you ask, you will only elicit their complaints.

74. A grave-robber who repented to God* reported that he said to his spiritual master one day: "Master, I robbed a thousand graves and found the faces of their inhabitants all turned away from the direction of prayer." His Master replied: "My son, that was because of their doubts regarding their provisions."

75. O servant of God, if you ask God for anything, ask Him to restore you in every way and that He restore you by making you pleased with the manner in which He disposes your affairs.

70. *J.K.*, 61 alone has *al-jamal* (the camal).

76. But you are a renegade servant. He asks you to come over to Him, but you flee instead. And fleeing can be by deeds, spiritual states, or degree of spiritual ambition. When you are unmindful in your prayer, full of prattle during your fast and given to complaining in the face of God's kindness, are you not a renegade?

77. On the authority of Shaykh Abū al-Ḥasan al-Shādhilī°: "Once I spent three days in the desert, unable to find my way to any provisions.[71] Some Christians passed by and saw me in repose and said, 'This is a holy man from among the Muslims.' Then they placed some food near my head and left. I said, 'How strange it is that I should be provided for at the hands of adversaries while I was not provided for by loved ones.' It was said, 'The true man is not one who is provided for by loved ones; the true man is one who is provided for by adversaries.'"

78. Good sir, treat your self like you treat your pack animal: every time it veers away from the path, you strike it so that it returns. If only you would treat your self like you treat your outer garment, you would achieve happiness: as soon as it gets dirty you wash it; and as soon as it gets torn you mend and restore it.

79. Many a man is there whose beard turns white, while he has yet to have a single audience with God in which he calls himself to account. Shaykh Makīn al-Dīn al-Asmar° said: "In the beginning I used to call myself to account every night. I would say, 'Today I said this and that.' And I would find that I spoke three or four words. One day there was a *shaykh* in his presence who was about ninety years old to whom he said: 'Master, I wish to express to you my dissatisfaction with the plentitude of my sins.' The shaykh responded, 'This is something of which we have no knowledge. I do not know that I have ever committed a sin.'"

71. *I.Q.*, 38, *J.K.*, 63: *lam yuftaḥ lī shay'*; *Shaqrūn*, 19, *N.K.*, 66: *lam yaṣiḥḥa lī shay'*.

80. Just as there are people of worldly acumen who suffice anyone who relies on them, there are people of otherworldly acumen who relieve the needs of anyone who relies on them. And do not say, "I have sought such people but not found them." For, were you to seek in earnest, you would find them. The reason that you do not find them is that you are not properly prepared. For the bride is not revealed to profligates. Were you really seeking to behold the bride,[72] you would abandon profligate behavior. And were you to abandon profligate behavior, you would see the saints, who are many and whose numbers do not decrease[73]. For, were they to decrease even by one, the light of prophethood would decrease in like proportion.

81. If you fall in love with someone, you cannot (expect to) gain access to them until you are worthy of such. And that is the case that you might purify yourself of your indiscretions. Shaykh Abū al-Ḥasan al-Shādhilī° said: "God's saints are like brides, and criminals do not get to see brides."

82. When obedience and proper worship become heavy upon you and cease to be accompanied by any sweetness in your heart and when disobedience becomes easy for you and is accompanied by such sweetness, know that you have not been sincere in your repentance. For, were the tree sound, so too would be its fruit.[74]

83. Would that you obeyed your Lord as your servant obeys you. You like to see the latter perpetually exerting himself in your service. You, on the other hand, admire obedience but seek to exit from it as quickly as you can, prostrating like a bird pecking the earth with its beak.

72. *N.K.*, 69 adds here *yā maghrūr* (O deluded one).

73. *N.K.*, 69 adds "*wa lā yanqati' madaduhum*" (and their aid does not cease).

74. Literally, "were the root sound, so too would be the branch." This last sentence, incidentally, does not appear in *J.K.*, 66.

Would that you had a vision by which to observe the beauties of things other than yourself to compensate for your (spiritual) blindness.[75]

84. How often humiliation comes to you as a result of your groveling at the doorsteps of humans. How often they humiliate you, yet you do not return to your Lord.

85. On the authority of Shaykh Makīn al-Dīn al-Asmar°: "I saw one of the women of Paradise in a dream. She said to me, 'I am for you and you are for me.' Her words were so sweet that after that I went two or three months unable to listen to the words of earthly humans without vomiting."

86. It is enough turning your back (on the truth) that you open your eyes to the vanities of this abode. God* says, "*Do not extend your eyes to the comforts We have provided groups among them as adornments of the life of this world, that We may try them thereby.* [20:131]

87. He has decreed your health and sickness, your wealth and poverty, your happiness and sadness, that you may know Him by His attributes.

88. Anyone who spends a day or two with you without seeing any benefit in you will abandon you and spend their time with someone else. You have spent forty years with your self without seeing any benefit in it. Thus, say to it, "Return, O self, to pursuing the pleasure of your Lord. How long I have gone along with you in seeking to satisfy your carnal desires!" Substitute (spiritual) laziness with preoccupation with God, talkativeness with silence, groveling at the doorsteps of others with sitting alone in solitude,[76] enjoying the intimacy of humans with enjoying the intimacy of God, keeping

75. *J.K.*, 66 has *al-'umr*, while *I.Q.* 40, *Shaqrūn*, 20, and *N.K.*, 70 read *al-'amā*.

76. *I.Q.*, 41: *wa ba'da al-wuqūf bi al-abwāb al-julūs bi al-khalwah; Shaqrūn*, 21, *N.K.*, 72: *wa ba'da al-wuqūf bi al-ḥārāt al-julūs bi al-khalwah; J.K.*, 67: *wa ba'da al-wuqūf bi al-abwāb wa al-ḥārāt al-julūs bi al-khalwah.*

company with the wicked with staying in the company of the good and righteous.

89. Do everything the opposite of what you used to. Instead of staying up at night in disobedience to God, stay up in obedience to Him. Instead of seeking the company of worldly people, turn away from them and seek the company of God. Instead of paying attention to their speech, listen and pay attention to the speech of God*. Instead of eating with gluttony and craving, eat little, just enough to sustain you in remaining obedient to God. God* said, "*Those who strive in Our way, We will guide them indeed to Our paths.*" [29: 69]

90. It is simply one who does not know the punishment of God who will disobey Him. And it is simply one who does not know the reward of God who refuses to obey Him. Had they knowledge of God's punishment, they would not be heedless. And had they knowledge of what God has prepared for the people of Paradise, they would not for a second abandon obedience to Him.

91. When you keep company with worldly people, they draw you to the life of this world. When you keep company with otherworldly people, they draw you to God. The Prophet* said, "A person imbibes the religion of his intimate friends, so let him be careful about whom he takes as an intimate friend." Just as you choose wholesome food that is free of harmful ingredients to eat and just as you choose a beautiful woman to marry, seek intimate friendship only with those who can give you knowledge of the path to God*.[77] And know that in reality you have but three intimate friends: (1) your money—which you will lose at death; (2) your family—who will leave you at the site of your grave; and (3) your deeds—which

77. *N.K.*, 75 adds *lā taṣḥab illā man yunhiḍuka ḥāluhu wa yadulluka ʿalā Allāh maqāluh* (And do not keep company with anyone save one whose comportment motivates you and whose discourse directs you toward God).

will never leave you. So start now cultivating companionship and getting intimate with the one that will enter the grave with you. Indeed, the reasonable person is the person who understands God's commands and prohibitions as imparted by God.

92. You are like a dung beetle. It lives in feces and waste, and when a rose is brought near it, it dies from its sweet scent. There are people who resemble dung beetles in their spiritual ambition and moths in their intellect. Moths repeatedly cast themselves into the fire until it burns them. In a similar fashion, you deliberately cast yourself into the fire of disobedience. And had it been your desire to make your way to God*, you would have tightened your belt. But, alas, where is spiritual ambition?

93. You eat to live and live to eat.[78] In so doing, you resemble many of those who descend upon feeding troughs,[79] as you do many animals. If this is what you do, (you should remember that) the lean horse is fastest. (But, alas) you say, "Tonight I am going to limit my intake of food." But when the food arrives,[80] it is greeted like a long lost friend.

94. Whomever God does not will to make righteous, words will merely exhaust themselves on them. God* says, "*And whomever God wills to try, you will not be able to divert anything of God's trials away from them.*" [5: 41]

95. How desperately you flee from humiliation, and how hopelessly prone to it you remain. You humiliate yourself and cast it into places where ruin awaits. Said one of them, "Be with God like a child

78. *Shaqrūn*, 22; *J.K.*, 69; *N.K.*, 76: *innamā ta'kul li ta'īsh wa ta'īsh li ta'kul*; *I.Q.*, 43: *innamā ta'kul li ta'īsh wa lā ta'īsh li ta'kul*, i.e., "You eat to live but do not live to eat," presumably the delights of the Afterlife.

79. *J.K.*, 69; *N.K.*, 76: *fa mithāluka 'alā al-madhāwid*; *I.Q.*, 43, *Shaqrūn*, 22: *fa mithāluka 'alā al-madāwid*.

80. *N.K.*, 77 adds here *bayna yadayk* (in front of you).

with his mother: every time she nudges him away he throws himself into her embrace, oblivious to everything but her."

96. O servant of God, you are careful in selecting good things for yourself, even the fodder you select for your animals. Yet, you take chances in your interactions with God. You might examine twenty watermelons before finding one good enough to fill the inside of your toilet. You sit up straight at the table and may even tarry when you eat. But when it comes to prayer you prostrate like a rooster pecking the earth, devilish whisperings and vile thoughts inundating you all the while.[81] Such a person is like one who sets himself up as a stationary target and then sits there while spears and arrows come at him from every direction. Is not such a person an idiot?

97. When you hear wisdom but do not act on it,[82] you are like a person who puts on armor but does not fight. Has not the call gone out announcing our wares? Are there any buyers?

98. Your value is the value of that with which you occupy yourself. If you are consumed by the life of this world, you have no value; for the life of this world is like a corpse: it has no value.

99. The best thing a person can ask God for is to make him upright in his dealings with God. God* said (instructing the believers on supplication in this regard), "*Guide us along the straight path.*" [1: 6] So, ask God for guidance and uprightness. And that is to be at all times in a state in which it would please God to find you, in accordance with what the Prophet*[83] related from God*.

81. *N.K.*, 78 adds *wa anta muḥrim* (while you are in a sacred state of prayer).
82. *I.Q.*, 44; *Shaqrūn*, 22: *mā mithāluka idhā sami'ta al-ḥikmah wa lam ta'mal bihā*; *N.K.*, 78: *mithāluka idhā sami'ta al-ḥikmah wa lam ta'mal bihā*; *J.K.*, 71: *mā sha'nuka in asma'ta al-ḥikmah wa lam ta'mal bihā*.
83. *N.K.*, 79 adds *al-mukarram*.

100. Whoever expends pure love for God, God will serve them from the cup of pure generosity.

101. The traveler on the spiritual path is like one who digs in search of water little by little until he finds a hole from which water springs as a result of his effort.[84] One who is actually attracted to God, however, is like one over whom a rain cloud opens, such that he is able to take what he needs without toil.

102. When you grant your self all that it craves and seeks of carnal pleasures, you are like a person who has a snake in his house which he fattens every day to the point that it devours him. Had God granted you a spirit without a self, you would have obeyed Him and never disobeyed. Had He granted you a self without a spirit, you would have disobeyed Him and never obeyed. This is why you vacillate.[85] Thus, He gave you a heart, a spirit, a self, and undisciplined passions, like a bee in whom He deposits a sting and honey,[86] the honey as a manifestation of His kindness, the sting as a manifestation of His might.[87] God wanted to temper the provocations of the self through the presence of the heart and the inhibitions of the heart through the presence of the self.

103. O servant of God, He[88] requested that you be a servant of His but you refused to be but the opposite. To devote yourself to[89] God is to single Him out as the sole object of worship. How, then, could He be pleased by your worship of others. Were you to

84. *Shaqrūn*, 23; *N.K.*, 80; *J.K.*, 72: *ḥattā yajid al-thaqb fa yanbaʿ lahu al-māʾ baʿda al-ṭalab*; *I.Q.*, 45: *ḥattā yajid al-māʾ baʿda al-taʿb*.

85. *I.Q.*, 46; *N.K.*, 80, *J.K.*, 72: *fa li dhālika tatalawwan*; *I.Q.*, 46, nt. 1 intimates, however, that this is awkward, apparently taking *talawwan* in its literal sense, "to turn colors."

86. Between here and the next line, *Shaqrūn*, 23 and *N.K.*, 80 has *fa li dhālika tatalawwan*; *J.K.*, 72 has *fa li dhālika talawwan*. *I.Q.*, 46 nt. 1 indicates that this is what their printed edition has.

87. *I.Q.*, 46; *Shaqrūn*, 23: *fa al-ʿasal bi birrih wa al-lasʿ bi qahrih*; *N.K.*, 80: *fa al-ʿasal yabarruhu wa al-lasʿ yaqharuh*; *J.K.*, 72: *fa al-ʿasal yubirruhu wa al-lasʿ yaqharuh*.

88. *N.K.*, 81 adds *mawlāka* (your Master).

89. *N.K.*, 81 adds *ghayr* (other than).

approach us seeking undue generosity, this would not be fair. How much more unfair would it be should you then devote yourself to others instead of us?[90]

104. [91]The life of this world stands in your path to the Afterlife and diverts you away from it. The Afterlife stands in your path to God and denies you access to Him.[92]

105. It is out of God's benevolence toward you that He reveals your faults to you while concealing them from the people.[93]

106. When you are granted worldly comforts but are denied (the blessing of) gratitude, what you have been granted becomes a trial for you. The Prophet* said, "A little worldly comfort can distract one from the path to the Afterlife."[94]

107. One of them had a wife who said to him one day, "I cannot stand your being away from me nor your heart being preoccupied with other than me." A voice cried out, "If she who is neither a Creator nor a Producer should love that your heart be focused on her, how could I not love that your heart be focused on Me?"

90. *I.Q.*, 46; *N.K.*; 81, *J.K.*, 73: *fa law ataytanā taṭlub al-ʿaṭāʾ minnā mā anṣaftanā fa kayfa idhā aqbalta ʿalā man siwānā*; *Shaqrūn*, 23: *fa law ataytanā taṭlub al-ʿaṭāʾ minnā mā anṣaftanā fa kayfa tarḍā idhā aqbalta ʿalā man siwānā.*

91. *J.K.*, 73 adds here *idhā aqbalta ʿalā man siwānā.*

92. *N.K.*, 81; *Shaqrūn*, 23: *waqafat al-dunyā fī ṭarīq al-ākhirah fa ṣarafat al-wuṣūl ilayhā wa waqafat al-ākhirah fī ṭarīq al-ḥaqq fa manaʿat al-wuṣūl ilayhi*; *I.Q.*, 46: *waqafta al-dunyā fī ṭarīq al-ākhirah fa ṣarafta al-wuṣūl ilayhā wa waqafta al-ākhirata fī ṭarīq al-ḥaqq fa muniʿta al-wuṣūl ilayhi*; *J.K.*, 72: *waqafta al-dunyā fī ṭarīq al-ākhirah fa ṣurifta al-wuṣūl ilayhā wa waqafta al-ākhirata fī ṭarīq al-ḥaqq fa muniʿta al-wuṣūl ilayhi.* The idea here is apparently that just as a surfeited pursuit of material comfort in this life can divert one away from the Afterlife, a surfeited pursuit of the comforts of the Afterlife can divert one from the real goal of religion: an organic relationship with God! Note also that none of *Shaqrūn*'s text is voweled, and I have therefore assumed his voweling to be the same as *N.K.*, though it could also be consistent with that of *I.Q.* or *J.K.*

93. *N.K.*, 81 adds *wa yaṣduq ʿalayhi qawl al-nabī ṣalla Allāh ʿalayhi wa sallama idhā aḥabba Allāh ʿabdan baṣṣarahu bi ʿuyūb nafsih* (and the statement of the Prophet* applies to him, "When God loves a person, He grants them insight into their own flaws").

94. This entire sentence in omitted from *N.K.*, 82.

108. I was once with[95] Shaykh Abū al-ʿAbbās al-Mursī (d. 686/1287)°. I said, "There are things brewing in my self." The Shaykh responded, "If your self belongs to you, then do with them as you please. But you will not be able to do that." Then he said, "The self is like a woman, the more you argue with it, the more it will argue with you. So surrender it to its Lord and let Him do with it as He pleases. Indeed, you may tire to exhaustion in your attempt to train your self, and it may still not yield. The Muslim is one who surrenders his self to God, and the proof of this is The Exalted's statement, '*Verily God has purchased from the believers their souls and their possessions in exchange for Paradise.*'" [9: 111]

109. When your Master loves you, He turns your companions away from you so that they don't distract you away from Him. And He severs your attachments to the people, so that you may return to Him.

110. How often you ask your self to obey but it merely slumps in refusal. You simply need to initiate a course of treatment[96] for your self from the ground up. When it eventually comes to taste the grace of God, it will respond voluntarily, and the sweetness it used to find in disobedience it will go back to finding in obedience.

111. Faith in the heart is like a leafy tree: if disobedience engulfs it, it dries up and ceases to provide benefit. So, whoever wants to be able to fulfill his obligations, let him abandon forbidden acts. And whoever abandons discouraged acts will be assisted in attaining good things. Whoever abstains from even neutrally permitted things, God will grant him an abundance that his mind is unable to fathom and admit him to His presence. And

95. *J.K.*, 74, nt. 1 indicates that *kuntu marrah ʿinda* is missing from his manuscript source. This appears in both *I.Q.* and *Shaqrūn*.

96. *I.Q.*, 48; *Shaqrūn*, 24, *N.K.*, 84: *muʿālajah*; *J.K.*, 75: *muṣālaḥah*.

whoever abandons listening to that which is forbidden, God will enable him to hear His word.[97]

112. But how easy those acts of drawing near to God are via which your self satisfies some passion. And how difficult those are in which there is no such satisfaction. For example, you might perform a supererogatory pilgrimage. But if it is said to you, "Make a charitable donation of equal worth," this will weigh heavily upon you. This is because pilgrimage is seen among men, and thus the self has a share in it. Charitable donations, on the other hand, are quickly devoured and forgotten. Likewise is your pursuit of knowledge for other than God's sake. You stay up all night studying, and your self is content. But if it is said to you, "Pray two units," this will weigh heavily upon you. This is because the two units of prayer are between you and God* and the self has no share in them. Reading and studying, on the other hand, offer the self the pleasure of communing with others. For this reason, it is light on the self.[98]

113. Said one of them, "My self yearned for marriage. But then I saw a cleft open up in the prayer niche from which a golden shoe decked out in pearls emerged. It was said to me, 'This is her shoe, so what of her face?' At that point, the desire to get married fell from my heart."

114. It is not fitting for one for whom the stations of ascension have been set up that he should languish at garbage dumps. Perform good deeds between you and God in secret,[99] and do not allow even

97. *N.K.*, 85: *wa man taraka istimāʿ mā ḥurrima ʿalayhi istimāʿuh*; *I.Q.*, 48, *Shaqrūn*, 24: *wa man taraka istimāʿ mā ḥaruma ʿalayhi kalāmuh*." *I.Q.*, 48, nt. 3 states that their printed edition has ʿ*qalla kalāmuh* in place of *kalāmuh*.

98. We have heard from al-Shādhilī on this point. One is also reminded here of what the Spaniard Ibrāhīm b. Mūsā al-Shāṭibī refers to as "barely perceptible carnal desire" (*al-shahwah al-khafīyah*), in which he includes the pleasures of the life of the mind and the sense of conquest that intellectual discoveries induce. See his *al-Muwāfaqāt fī uṣūl al-sharīʿah*, 4 vols. ed. ʿA. Drāz (Cairo: al-Maktabah al-Tijārīyah al-Kubrā, N.d.), 1: 67–68.

99. *N.K.*, 86 deletes *sirran* (in secret).

your family to know about them. Make these your stored provisions with God; you will find them on the Day of Judgment. Indeed, the self derives a certain satisfaction from remembering one's good deeds. One of them fasted forty years[100] and his family never knew anything about it.

115. Do not expend the breaths you draw on disobedience to God. And do not look at the smallness of individual breaths.[101] Rather, look at their significance and to what God brings to people through them. The breaths you draw are jewels. Do you see anyone[102] who throws jewels in the garbage?

116. Shall you restore your outward appearance while corrupting your inner being? Your likeness is that of a leper who wears fine clothing while pus and matter flow beneath. You restore that which the people observe,[103] but you do not restore your heart, which is for your Lord.

117. Wisdom is like a bridle. If you use it to restrain your self, the latter will yield. But if you discard it, your self will proceed with abandon and your fate will be dreaded. It is like having a mad person in your home who destroys furnishings and rips up clothing. If you restrain him, you will be spared his destructions. But if you simply remove his restrainer and leave the house, the havoc he wreaks will persist.

118. My aging sir, your life is now spent, so make amends for what has escaped you. You have donned whiteness, i.e., white hair, and whiteness is most sensitive to stains (of disobedience).

100. *N.K.*, 86–87 adds *lam yufṭir bihā siwā al-ʿīdayn* (only eating during that time in honor of Eid celebrations).

101. *I.Q.*, 50: *ṣighar al-nafas*; *Shaqrūn*, 25; *N.K.*, 87; *J.K.*, 76–77: *ṣaghīr al-nafas*.

102. *N.K.*, 87 adds *min al-ʿuqalāʾ* (among rational people).

103. *I.Q.*, 50; *Shaqrūn*, 25: *fa anta tuṣliḥ mā yanẓur ilayi al-nās*: *N.K.*, 87: *fa anta tuṣliḥ mā yanẓur al-nās ilayh*; *J.K.*, 77: *fa anta tuṣliḥ qālibaka wa huwa mā yanẓur ilayhi al-nās*.

119. The heart is like a mirror, and the self is like breath. Every time you breathe on a mirror, you impair it. The heart of a corrupt person[104] is like the mirror of a crone who is too disinterested to clean and look in it. The heart of one who is gifted with supersensory knowledge, however, is like the mirror of a fresh young bride who looks at it every day and keeps it polished.

120. The ambitions of ascetics are directed toward augmenting good deeds. The ambitions of those of supersensory knowledge are directed toward policing the states of their souls. Four things, however, will aid you in clearing your heart: (1) constant remembrance; (2) observing silence; (3) solitude; and (4) minimal food and drink. When people of heedlessness awake, they check their money. People of asceticism and worship check the states of their souls. People of supersensory knowledge check the condition of their hearts with God*.

121. God* simply wants to test you with every breath of obedience, illness, or poverty He brings forth in you. Whoever seeks worldly gain by feigning pursuit of the Afterlife is like one who uses an emerald spoon to scoop feces. Would not such a person be counted an idiot?

122. Do not think that it is knowledge that has escaped the people. It is more divine facilitation than knowledge that has escaped them.

123. The first thing you should do is cry over your faculty of reasoning. For, just as drought befalls open pastures it befalls the minds of men. It is through reason that people are able to live with each other and with God*: with each other through good morals; with God through pursuing His pleasure.

104. *I. Q.*, 51, nt., 1 states that "a printed version has *qalb al-ʿājiz*" ("the heart of the impotent"). *Shaqrūn*, 26; *N.K.*, 89, and *J.K.*, 77, however, are the same as *I.Q.*

124. If God gifts you with three things, He gifts you with the greatest bounty: (1) observing His limits; (2) fulfilling your covenants with Him; and (3) immersion in witnessing His presence.

125. The only reason you marvel at the states of those of supersensory knowledge is that you are overwhelmed by disconnectedness. Had you shared their journeys, you would share their experiences. And had you shared their hardship,[105] you would share their happiness.

126. At those times when your self is pleased, it is simply like a theretofore fettered camel: when you unfetter it, it dashes off. The Prophet* said, "The human heart is even more severe in its fluctuations than a pot boiling on a fire." How many people's connection with God is broken in a single breath! And how many people go to sleep in obedience to God only to awake and enter a state of disconnectedness!

127. The heart is like the eye. It is not the entire eye through which we see but simply the diameter of the lens. Likewise the heart: it is not the fleshy entity that is important but the subtle something that God places in it through which we apprehend reality. God has suspended the heart off to the left side of the chest like a dangling bucket. When the winds of carnal desire blow upon it, they sway it in one direction. When the winds of God-conscious impulses blow upon it, they sway it in another. Sometimes capricious impulses dominate, and sometimes God-conscious impulses dominate, that God may show you now His graciousness, now His overwhelming power. Sometimes He grants victory to God-conscious impulses, that He may praise you. And sometimes He

105. Rather than *al-'anā'*, "hardship," as in *I.Q.*, 53, *Shaqrūn*, 27, *N.K.*, 92 and *J.K.*, 81, the editors of *I.Q.* (53, nt. 1) report that the manuscript from which they are working has *al-fanā'*, "spiritual annihilation," according to which one loses oneself in the divine.

grants victory to capricious impulses, that He may censure you. The heart, then, is like a roof inside a house: if fires are lighted in the house, its fumes will rise to the roof and blacken it. Likewise with carnal desire: if it germinates in the body, its gases will rise to the heart and blacken it.

128. When the powerful[106] wrong you, repair to The All-Powerful. And do not fear the powerful, lest they be granted power over you.

129. One who sees the ultimate source of his problems in created beings is like a dog whom a man hits with a brick and then the dog goes and bites the brick, not knowing that the brick has no agency of its own. Such a person and this dog are equal. One who sees the ultimate source of the favors he enjoys in created beings is like a horse who, when its trainer approaches shakes its tail in happiness. But when its owner approaches, it pays him no attention. If you are intelligent, see God* as the ultimate source of things, and do not see this in anything else.

130. The lost one is not one who loses his way in the desert. The lost one is one who is unable to find the path to guidance. You seek honor from people, but you do not seek it from God. But one who seeks honor from the people has lost his way. And one who has lost his way will only be taken farther from his desired destination the longer he travels on that road. This is truly the lost one.

131. If you say, "There is no god but God," God will demand of you that you live up to this and recognize its true meaning. That means that you do not attribute the ultimate cause of things to anyone but God.

132. When you deliver the heart to the self, it is like a person who grabs onto another who is drowning: both of them drown. But

106. *Shaqrūn*, 27: *idhā ẓalamaka al-qawī*; *I.Q.*, 54, *N.K.*, 94: *idhā ẓalamaka al-ghawī* (a wanton person); *J.K.*, 83: *idhā ẓalamaka qawī (al-makhlūq)* [*sic*].

when you surrender the self to the heart, it is like a person who gives himself over to a master swimmer[107] who delivers him to safety. Do not be like one who surrenders his heart to his self. Do you see a person who can see giving himself over to be led by the blind?

133. If you are able to wake up and go to sleep without wronging anyone, you have achieved success. And if you do not wrong yourself concerning that which is between you and God, your success is all the more complete. Close your eyes, plug your ears, and never, ever wrong people!

134. [108]In your smallness of mind and lack of knowledge of how sheltered you are, you are no different from a child whose mother dresses him in the most beautiful and finest clothing, while he remains clueless. He may even soil and defile these garments, at which time his mother will rush to clothe him in something else, so that people do not see him like this. She purifies what he defiles, while he, due to the smallness of his mind, has no idea of what has been done for him.

135. Shaykh Abū al-Ḥasan al-Shādhilī° said: "It was said to me, 'O Alī, cleanse your clothing of impurities, you will enjoy[109] assistance from God in every breath.' I said, 'What are my clothing?' It was said, 'God clothed you in a robe of supersensory knowledge, then a robe of monotheism, then a robe of love, then a robe of faith, then a robe of submission.[110] One who knows God finds everything else insignificant. And one who loves God finds every undertaking

107. *I.Q.*, 55: *fa sallamahā*; *N.K.*, 96: *fa sallimhā lahu*; *Shaqrūn*, 28, *J.K.*, 84: *fa sallamahā lahu* or *fa sallimhā lahu*.

108. *N.K.*, 97 adds *yā hādhā* (good sir).

109. *I.Q.*, 56; *J.K.*, 85: *taḥẓa madad Allāh*; *Shaqrūn*, 28; *N.K.*, 97: *tuḥfaẓ bi madad Allāh*.

110. *I.Q.*, 56; *Shaqrūn*, 28; *N.K.*, 98: *inna Allāh kasāka ḥullat al-ma'rifah thumma ḥullat al-tawḥīd thumma ḥullat al-maḥabbah thumma ḥullat al-īmān thumma ḥullat al-islām*; *J.K.*, 85: *inna Allāh kasāka ḥullat al-ma'rifah thumma ḥullat al-tawḥīd thumma ḥullat al-maḥabbah thumma ḥullat al-tawfīq thumma ḥullat al-īmān thumma ḥullat al-islām*.

simple and easy. One who recognizes God's unity will not associate anything with Him. And one who has faith in God is secure from every threat. One who surrenders to God rarely disobeys Him, and if he does, he begs God's pardon. And if he begs God's pardon, God will pardon him.'" He said, "I understood from this the meaning of God's statement, "*And your clothing purify*!" [74: 4]

136. O you who are alive but have not lived, you exit from this world without tasting the sweetest thing in it: communion with God* and His addressing you. It is as if you have been discarded as a corpse in the night. If you are denied this benefit, seek assistance from God and say, "O angels of God, O messenger of my Lord,[111] I missed the benefit of the sweetness of communion and the intimate love of openhearted friendship that others received."

137. When a person is conceited about his obedience to God, arrogant toward God's creatures, full of self-aggrandizement, demanding that people recognize his rights while he does not recognize theirs, it is feared that such a person will meet a disastrous end—may God protect us from that. But if when he commits an act of disobedience, you see him weeping, sad, broken, and humiliated, throwing himself at the feet of the righteous, visiting them, and acknowledging his shortcomings, there is reason to hope that such a person will meet a favorable end.[112]

138. If you are looking for a Qur'ān reciter, you will find that they are countless. If you are looking for a doctor, you will find that they too are many. If you are looking for a jurist, you will find that they are equally numerous. But if you are looking for someone who will direct you to God and disclose your faults to

111. *I.Q.*, 56; *Shaqrūn*, 29, *N.K.*, 99: *yā malā'ikat Allāh yā rasūla rabbī*; *J.K.*, 85–86: *yā malā'ikata rabbī yā rasūla rabbī*.

112. *N.K.*, 100 adds *in shā' Allāh ta'ālā* (if God The Exalted wills).

you, you will find that such people are few. So, if you are fortunate enough to find such a person, hold fast to them with both hands!

139. If you want to be aided to victory, be completely humble. God* said, "*And God aided you to victory at Badr while you were humble.*" [3:123] If you want to be given charity, be completely poor: "*Charity is simply for the poor and needy.*" [9: 60]

140. [113]You find yourself thirsty in the middle of a river. You find yourself groping for connectedness while you are with Him in the middle of a religious gathering. It is as if people (think that they) cannot make it[114] to the Afterlife except through plenty of food and drink or as if they have been told, "These are the things that will get you to the Afterlife." But how little you value yourself! For were it not so insignificant to you, you would not expose it to the punishment of God*. How precious, on the other hand, your self is to you when it comes to pursuing and piling up the vanities of this world. And how absolutely amazing it is that one will consult an astrologer about his condition but will not consult the Book of God or the Sunna of God's Prophet*!

141. If you are too spiritually weak to worship as you should, mend the holes in your worship with weeping and humble beseeching. If you are asked, "Over whom should one weep?" say, "Over a person who was restored to health and spent it on disobedience to God."

142. If you go to sleep in a state of ritual dishevelment, you will see tumultuous things in your dreams. You should sleep in a state of ritual purity and repentance, that God may open your heart by His light. But alas, one who is consumed by hollow vanities during the day will not be mindful of God at night.

113. At this point, *J.K.*, 87 jumps to what I have translated from ¶ 185 all the way up to the third sentence of ¶ 201, i.e., to *J.K.*, 93. This is in contradistinction to *I.Q.*, *Shaqrūn*, and *N.K.*

114. *I.Q.*, 57, *Shaqrūn*, 29, *J.K.*, 93: *lam yatawāṣalū*; *N.K.*, 101: *lam yatahayya'ū.*

143. If you see one of God's* saints, do not allow your reverence of him to keep you from sitting in his presence, with proper etiquette, and seeking his blessings. And know that heaven and earth show proper etiquette before the saints, just as people do.

144. Whoever rejoices when the pleasures of this life approach him has established that he is an idiot. An even bigger idiot, however, is one who is saddened when these things pass him by. In so doing, you are like a person to whom a snake comes to bite but then moves on. God* saves him from this snake, but he is saddened by the fact that the latter did not harm him.

145. Among the signs of heedlessness and lack of intelligence is that you worry about possible occurrences while ignoring occurrences that are certain. You wake up saying, "What will the price[115] of such and such be tomorrow? What will conditions be this year?" All the while God's facilitations buoy you in ways that you could never fathom. But doubt regarding one's provisions is doubt regarding The Provider. The thief and the robber only steal and rob what they were destined to receive. Indeed, as long as you are alive, your provisions will not fall below what you were destined to receive.

146. It is ignorant enough of you that you worry about insignificant things while ignoring major matters. Worry about whether you will die as a Muslim or as a nonbeliever! Worry about whether your ultimate end will be miserable or happy! Worry about the Hellfire that is described as everlasting and has no end! Worry about whether you will receive your Record of Deeds in your right or left hand![116] These are the things about which you should worry. Don't worry

115. *I.Q.*, 59, *N.K.*, 104, *J.K.*, 95: *kayfa yakūn al-si'r*; *Shaqrūn*, 30: *kayfa yakūn al-safar*.

116. A reference to several verses in the Qur'ān in which receipt of one's record of deeds in one's right hand is an indication of successfully passing God's judgment. See, e.g., 17: 71, 69: 19; 84: 7.

about your daily bread and water![117] Shall the King employ you but not feed you? Shall you be put up in the hospitality suite but then be left to waste away?

147. The most beloved manifestation of obedience to God is trust in Him.[118]

148. That you be undistinguished in this world is better for you than being undistinguished[119] on the Day of Judgment.

149. This world is a strainer and sifter of life. O you who will only eat wheat that is sifted, your deeds will also have to be sifted, such that the only ones that remain in your favor are those in whose execution you were sincere, everything else being cast aside. (In this context) the thing to be most feared for you is mixing with people. For it is not enough[120] that you hear their transgressions with your ears, you end up participating with them in their backbiting,[121] which invalidates one's ablution and violates one's fast.

150. It is ignorant enough of you that you are zealously vigilant regarding your wife but not regarding your faith. It is treacherous enough that you vigilantly monitor her, in the interest of your self, but not your heart, in the interest of your Lord. If you are going to protect that which is for you, will you not protect that which is for your Lord?

151. If you see a person who wakes up in the morning worried about his provisions, know that this person is far removed from God. Indeed, were some mere mortal to say to you, "Do not preoccupy yourself with the means of earning a living tomorrow; I will give you five silver *dirhāms*," you would trust him, though he is but a

117. *N.K.*, 105 adds *aw thawb talbasuh* (or clothing to wear).
118. *N.K.*, 105 adds *wa al-ittikāl ʿalayh* (and reliance upon Him).
119. *N.K.*, 105 adds *fī al-ākhirah* (in the Hereafter).
120. *I.Q.*, 60; *Shaqrūn*, 31, *J.K.*, 105: *wa lā yakfīka*; *J.K.*, 96: *a wa lā yakfīka*.
121. *N.K.*, 106 adds *wa namīmah* (sowing dissension).

contingent mortal. Will you not be sustained, then, by The Non-Contingent, The All-Generous who guarantees your provisions along with your appointed time?

152. A poet[122] once said:

When the twentieth day of Sha'bān turns and departs
Continue drinking during the day as you do at night
And do not drink from vessels that are small
For the times have become for small vessels too tight

153. The meaning of these lines, according to the poet, is that when the twentieth day of Sha'bān passes, we near the month of Ramadan, which will prevent us from drinking during the day. But for the people of the spiritual path, it means that when you pass the age of forty you should continue performing good deeds throughout the day and night,[123] because the time has drawn near for you to meet God*, and at this point, your deeds are not like those of a young man who has not wasted his youth and energy as you have wasted yours.

154. Assume that you want to get serious[124] but your powers will not assist you. Act in accordance with what your circumstances allow, and rectify the rest with remembrance. For there is nothing easier than that: you can do it standing, sitting, lying down, and even sick. Indeed, this is the easiest act of worship. This is the act about which the Prophet* said, "Let your tongue stay moist with remembrance of God."[125] And whatever supplication or expression

122. *I.Q.*, 60: *qāla al-shā'ir; Shaqrūn*, 31; *J.K.*, 107: *anshada insān; J.K.*, 97: *anshada insan shi'ran.*
123. *N.K.*, 107 adds *baqīyat ḥayātik* (for the rest of your life).
124. *N.K.*, 108 adds *fī al-a'māl al-ṣāliḥah* (about doing good deeds).
125. Related by al-Tirmidhī. See Muḥammad b. 'Abd al-Raḥmān b. 'Abd al-Raḥīm al-Mubārakfūrī, *Tuḥfat al-aḥwadhī bi sharḥ jāmi' al-tirmidhī*, 10 vols. (Beirut: Dār al-Kutub al-'Ilmīyah, N.d.), 9: 222.

of remembrance you find easy, persist in it. For whatever benefit it brings is from God*. Indeed, you will only be able to remember Him through His goodness and pleasure;[126] and you will only be turned away from Him by His dominance and might.

155. So work, and exert your every effort! (And remember), to be heedless in action is better than being heedless to the point of inaction. If you do this, your state of virtue will come to resemble that of the ascetics.[127] For the seeker does not desist from petitioning at the door. On the contrary, you find him there ever present, like a bereaved mother whose child has died. Do you see her attending weddings, reception parties, and banquets? On the contrary, she is preoccupied with the loss of her child!

156. How often the Master sends you His handiwork, while you act like a runaway slave. Your likeness is that of a child in a crib: whenever it is rocked, it sleeps. Were a king to send you a robe of honor, you would never awake any place except at his front door. So take advantage of the times of worship, and be steadfast in doing so.

157. If you seek to disobey Him, seek a place where no one can see you; and seek the power to disobey Him from other than Him. None of this will you be able to do; for all of this is from His bounty. Shall you take[128] of His bounty and then disobey Him by means thereof? But alas, you have mastered the art[129] of violating His commands, sometimes through backbiting, sometimes through sowing

126. *N.K.*, 108: *fa mā dhakartahu illā bi birrihi wa riḍāh*; *I.Q.*, 61, *Shaqrūn*, 32, *J.K.*, 99: *fa mā dhakartahu illā bi birrih.*

127. *Shaqrūn*, 32 has *tara*, in the jussive mood, which would render the following sentence the second half of a conditional begun by *fa''mal. I.Q.*, 61, *N.K.*, 109, *J.K.*, 99, on the other hand, all have *tarā* in the indicative mood.

128. *N.K.*, 110 adds *a yalīqu bika an* (is if fitting of you that).

129. *I.Q.*, 62; *Shaqrūn*, 32: *bal tafannanta fī al-mukhālafāt*; *J.K.*, 100: *bal tafannanta fī akhnā al-mukhālafāt*. *I.Q.*, 62, nt. 2 also reports that their manuscript has *tata'annat* for *tafannana*. *N.K.*, 110 has *tata'annat*.

dissension, sometimes through unlawfully gazing (at the opposite sex). What you have taken seventy years to build, you destroy in a single breath.

158. O nullifier of acts of obedience, God only saddles you with poverty in order for you to turn your affair over to Him and connect with Him. O you who inundates himself with carnal desires and acts of disobedience, would that you satisfied these through permissible means. But alas, how can you not love One whom you treat contemptuously while He treats you with benevolence? And how can you not love One who shows you generosity while you show Him nothing but ignobility?

159. No one befriends you in order to benefit you. Everyone simply befriends you to benefit his self. Your wife simply "loves" you in order to acquire through you decent food and clothing. Likewise your children, who say, "I will rely on him for support." Then, when you are old and have nothing of strength or desirables, they will all forsake you.[130]

160. Were you to sever your ties with people, God would open for you the door to intimacy with Him*. For God's saints are those who have overpowered their selves through solitude and isolation, in which state they are able to hear from God and enjoy intimacy with Him. So if you want to excavate the mirror of your heart out of the murky sludge, reject what they rejected, i.e., intimacy with the people and "What[131] befell so and so?" and "What happened with so and so?"[132] And do not languish on street corners. Whoever prepares himself will derive the benefit of preparation. And if He provides you

130. *I.Q.*, 63; *N.K.*, 111: *wa lā baqīyah rafaḍūk*; *Shaqrūn*, 33: *wa lā bughyah rafaḍuk*. *J.K.*,101: *wa lā baqīyah tarakūka wa rafaḍūk*.

131. *I.Q.*, 63; *J.K.*, 101: *aysh jarā*; *Shaqrūn*, 33, *N.K.*, 112: *uns jarā*.

132. *N.K.*, 112 has, *fa'rfuḍ mā rafaḍū wa'nus bi al-khalwah wa unsun jarā li fulān wa'ttafaqa li fulān*.

with the means of preparing yourself,[133] He will open the door for you to derive the benefit thereof. Whoever masters the proper way of knocking will have the door opened for him. But many a seeker simply knocks improperly, as a result of which they are turned away and the door is not opened for them, due to their lack of etiquette.

161. Peoples' greatest vulnerability is their lack of silence. Were you to gain closeness to[134] God, you would hear his address without interruption—in the market, in your house, etc. But it is simply he who is awake that is able to see. He who sleeps will neither hear via the ears of his heart nor see through his inner vision. Rather, the veil will be lowered over him.

162. If people really understood, they would devote themselves to none but God; nor would they sit in the presence of anyone but Him; nor would they seek fatwas from anyone but Him, in accordance with the statement of the Prophet*, "Ask your heart, even if they give you opinion upon opinion."[135] For divinely inspired thoughts[136] come from God, which means that they must be correct, while the mufti may err. The heart, on the other hand, is not susceptible to error. This applies, however, exclusively to pure hearts. (Otherwise) one should only seek fatwas from knowledgeable people. And those who are[137] heedless of God* have no knowledge.

133. I.Q., 63; *Shaqrūn*, 33; *N.K.*, 112: *idhā hayya'a laka*; *J.K.*, 101: *idhā hayya'aka*. According to *I.Q.*, 63, nt.3, their manuscript has *hayya'ta li al-isti'dād.*

134. *I.Q.*, 63; *Shaqrūn* 33; *N.K.*, 112: *fa law taqarrabta ilā Allāh*; *J.K.*, 102: *fa law fararta ilā Allāh*. According to *I.Q.*, 63, nt. 4, their manuscript has *nafarta*.

135. *I.Q.*, 64, nt. 1 indicates that this hadith appears in al-Bukhārī's *al-Tarīkh al-kabīr* and is commented on in al-Nawawī's *al-Arba'ūn*. They then note that al-Ghazālī stated in al-*Iḥyā'*, 2: 117–118: "How rare is such a heart! For this reason, the Prophet, upon him be peace, did not refer everyone to their own heart. He simply said this to Wāṣibah because of what he knew of the latter's state."

136. *Shaqrūn*, 33, *N.K.*, 113, *J.K.*, 102: *al-khawāṭir al-ilāhīyah*; *I.Q.*, 64: *al-khawāṭir al-ilhāmīyah*.

137. *N.K.*, 113 adds *qalbuh* (whose hearts are).

163. The Companions° would not enter into matters out of self-indulgence. They would enter, rather, in behalf of God and through reliance upon God. As the distance between the Companions and the saints widened, God made miracles a means of compensating for what the saints lacked in the way of following the Prophet directly. For this reason, some people have said, "The saints have miracles, while the Companions did not." Quite the contrary, however, the Companions had major miracles by virtue of their companionship with the Prophet*. Indeed, what miracle could be greater than that?

164. Know that every prayer that does not prevent obscene and reprehensible behavior should not be called a prayer, in accordance with God's statement, "*Verily prayer prevents obscene and reprehensible behavior*." [29: 45] But you exit from prayer and private communication with God* and the Prophet*—e.g., when you repeat the Qur'ānic phrase, "*Thee alone do we worship and Thine ultimate aid alone do we seek*" [1: 5] and when you say, "Peace be upon you, O Prophet, along with God's mercy and blessings," which you say in every prayer—and then go right back into sin, after all of these bounties that God has conferred upon you.

165. On the authority of Shaykh Abū al-Ḥasan al-Shādhilī°, who said that some of the jurists of Alexandria, along with the judge, used to visit him. They came to him once probing him on various matters. He instinctively detected their aim and said, "O jurists, O jurists, have you ever prayed? They replied, "O Shaykh, would any of us ever miss a prayer?" He said to them, "God* said, '*Verily humans were created anxious; when afflicted with evil they panic; and when blessed with good they withhold. Except those who pray*.' [70:19–22] Are you like this? When you are afflicted with evil, do you not panic? And when you are blessed with good, do you not withhold?" They all fell silent, at which time the Shaykh said to them, "Then, you have never prayed in the manner mentioned."

166. If He favors you with being able to repent to Him and you repent, this is a handsome gratuity from Him*. Indeed, you sin for seventy years and then repent to Him in a single breath, at which time He wipes out what you did during this entire period. "He who repents of a sin is as one who has committed no sin."[138] Every time a believer remembers his sinful acts, he is saddened. And every time he remembers his acts of obedience, he feels joy.

167. Luqmān the Wise[139] once said: "The believer is of two hearts, one with which he hopes and one with which he fears. He hopes that his deeds will be accepted, and he fears that they will not. Were the hope and fear of the believer placed on a scale, they would balance each other out."[140]

168. Whoever wants to connect with God, let him observe God's commands.

169. If you discover that your wife has betrayed you, she will become the object of your anger. Similarly, your self has betrayed you throughout your life. Now, reasonable people agree that a man does not harbor an unfaithful wife; rather he divorces her.[141] Thus, divorce your self!

170. The Prophet* was asked, "What most frequently causes people to enter Paradise?" He replied*, "God-consciousness and good character." It was then said to him, "What most frequently causes people to enter Hell?" He said, "The two repositories:[142] the mouth and the private parts."[143] Thus, wash your heart with regret over what you have forfeited from God*.

138. See Abū 'Abd Allāh Muḥammad b. Yazīd al-Qazwīnī, *Ṣaḥīḥ sunan ibn mājah*, 3 vols. Riyadh: Maktabat al-Ma'ārif li al-Nashr wa al-Tawzī' li Ṣāḥibihā Sa'd b. 'Abd al-Raḥmān Rāshid, 1417/1997), 3: 382.

139. An apparent reference to the Qur'ānic figure after whom *Sūrat Luqmān* is named.

140. See *I.Q.*, 66, nt. 3 for information on this report.

141. *N.K.*, 117 adds *al-ṭalāq al-thalāth* (thrice).

142. *N.K.*, 118 does not have *al-ajwafān* (the two repositories).

143. *J.K.*, 106, nt. 1 indicates that al-Tirmidhī, Ibn Mājah and Ibn Hibbān all relate this hadith.

171. By God, they err in wailing over a wife, a husband, a parent, or a child. Instead, they should wail over the absence of God-consciousness from their hearts.

172. [144]You laugh boisterously, as if you had already successfully crossed the bridge of *Ṣiraṭ*[145] and safely passed over[146] the Hellfire.

173. If there is not enough scrupulousness between you and God to prevent you from disobeying Him when you are alone,[147] throw dirt on your head, in accordance with the Prophet's statement, "Whoever does not have enough scrupulousness to prevent him from disobeying God when he is alone, God does not care about any of his deeds."[148]

174. [149]Nothing will embarrass you more on the Day of Judgment than a *dīnār* you spent on unlawful things.[150]

175. The important thing is not who is kind to you when you comply with them; the important thing is who is kind to you when you go against them. Among those things that are feared for you is your allying[151] yourself with sin to the point that He lures you through it into self-destruction, facilitating your ability to sin as you

144. *N.K.*, 118 adds *wāʿajabāhu laka* (How strange it is of you!).

145. Path between the judgment and paradise.

146. *Shaqrūn*, 35; *N.K.*, 118: *wa ʿathrat al-nīrān*; *J.K.*, 107: *ʿatharāt al-nīrān*; *I.Q.*, 68: *wa ʿabarta al-nīrān*.

147. *I.Q.*, 68; *Shaqrūn*, 35; *N.K.*, 118 and *J.K.*, 107 all have *wa illā fa ḍaʿ al-turāb ʿalā raʾsik*. I agree, however, with the editors of *I.Q.*, 68, nt. 1, that the addition of *illā* is simply a mistake.

148. *I.Q.*, 68; *Shaqrūn*, 35; *N.K.*, 119, and *J.K.*, 108: *lam yaʿbaʾ Allāh bi shayʾ min ʿamalih*; *J.K.*, 107: *lam yaʿbaʾ Allāh bi shayʾ min ʿilmih*. According to the editors of *I.Q.*, while this hadith does not appear in the canonical collections, Ibn ʿAsākir cited it in his *Tahdhīb tārīkh dimashq*, 2:65.

149. *N.K.*, 119 adds *waʿlam annahu* (Know that . . .).

150. This is what *I.Q.*, 68, *Shaqrūn*, 35, and *J.K.*, 119 all have. The editors of *I.Q.*, however, note that their manuscript has "Nothing will benefit you more on the Day of Judgment than a *dīnār* you spent on lawful things." See *I.Q.*, 68, nt. 2.

151. *Shaqrūn*, 35; *J.K.*, 108 and *N.K.*, 120 have *muwālāh*, with a singular feminine *tāʾ marbūtah*; *I.Q.*, 68 has *muwālāt* with a sound feminine plural ending.

please.[152] God* said, "*We will lure them to self-destruction in ways they perceive not.*" [68: 44]

176. If His providence[153] is with you, you will make do with little; if not, you will not make do even with a lot. Were He to lift the veil from you, you would see everything uttering the praises of God*. But both the defect and the veil reside in you.

177. How protective[154] you are of your body. But how cheap your religion is to you. Were it said to you, "This food is poisoned," you would refuse to eat it. Were someone then to swear to you on pain of divorcing his wife that it was actually not poisoned, you would still balk at it. In fact, were you yourself to wash the dish in which this food was contained several times, you would continue to shun it. Why are you not this way with your religion?[155]

178. How often God takes care of you better than your own mother did! When you were small, she took you and dressed you in the best clothing. And if you soiled them, she immediately brought you a new set. Now you come to a fabulous kingdom every inch of which is suitable for prostration. But you soil and wear out[156] your clothing with disobedience. This is what you do. Bounties abound all about you, but you contaminate them with disobedience.

179. Not everyone who remains in the company of great people is guided thereby. So don't make spending time with the *shaykhs* a cause for feeling secure. Whoever is deceived about God

152. *I.Q.*, 68; *Shaqrūn*, 35; *N.K.*, 120: *wa yumakkinaka minhā*; *J.K.*, 108: *wa yamnaʿaka min al-tawbah fīhā*.

153. *Shaqrūn*, 35; *N.K.*, 129; *J.K.*, 108: *ʿināyah*, without the third person pronoun, as in *I.Q.*, 68.

154. *I.Q.*, 69; *Shaqrūn*, 36; *N.K.*, 120: *iḥtirāsaka*; *J.K.*, 109: *iḥtirāzaka*. *I.Q.*, 69, nt. 1 reports that their manuscript has *iḥtirāzaka*.

155. *Shaqrūn*, 36; *J.K.*, 109; *N.K.*, 121: *fa lima lā takūn kadhālika fī dīnik*. *I.Q.*, 69: *fa lima takun kadhālika fī dīnik*. *I.Q.*, 69, nt. 2 reports, however, that both their manuscript and printed edition have "*fa lima takun kadhālika fī dīnik*."

156. *I.Q.*, 69; *Shaqrūn*, 36: *tutlif thawbaka*; *N.K.*, 12: *tutlif fīhā nafsak*; *J.K.*, 109: *takshif thawbaka*.

will disobey Him; for he entertains a false sense of security regarding His punishment. Thus, the ignorant say things like, "I accompanied master so and so," and "I saw master so and so." And they go on to make all kinds of false and baseless claims. If anything, the time they spent with the *shaykh*s should have increased them in fear and trembling. Indeed, the Companions[157] kept company with the Prophet*, and they were the greatest of people in fear and trembling.[158]

180. Wealth may constitute an impediment, while poverty may promote connectedness. For poverty compels you to implore God with humility. And poverty that connects you to God is better than wealth that cuts you off from Him.

181. Just as you have been commanded to turn away from disobedience, you have been commanded to turn away from those who disobey,[159] while secretly praying for their restoration. People today, however, do the opposite. But what good can your prayers and fasting do you, while you impugn the honor of your fellow Muslims?

182. The Prophet* said, "Renew your faith by saying, 'There is no god but God.'"[160] This indicates that the dust of disobedience and the defilement of violation will occasionally befall one's faith. But not every impurity can be removed with water. On the contrary, many an impurity can only be removed by fire, like gold when it is beset by impurities. This is how it will be with the disobedient of this Community: some will not qualify to enter Paradise until they are purified by the Hellfire.

157. *I.Q.*, 70; *J.K.*, 110: *fa qad ṣaḥaba al-ṣaḥābah rasūla Allāh*; *Shaqrūn*, 36; *N.K.*, 123: *fa qad ṣaḥaba al-mashāyikh rasūla Allāh*.

158. *J.K.*, 110: *wa kānū akthara al-nās wajalan wa makhāfatan*; *I.Q.*, 70; *Shaqrūn*, 36; *N.K.*, 123: *wa kānū akthara wajalan wa makhāfatan*.

159. *N.K.*, 123 adds *mawlāhu* (their Master).

160. *Musnad al-imām aḥmad*, 2: 359.

183. Only a person wrapped in the garments of God-consciousness should you envy.[161] This is the life. And how sweet the life of the lover with his beloved is when it is placed beyond watchful eyes. If a lover desires to be exposed to watchful eyes, he is not sincere in his love. Indeed, anyone who wants others to know his true state is deceived.

184. Do not be like those worldly people whom the world has divorced. Be, rather, among those who have divorced the world and parted *with it* before they depart *from it*. When you give preference to the life of this world, you are like a man who has two wives, one an unfaithful crone, the other a faithful young beauty. When you give preference to the unfaithful crone over the faithful young beauty, are you not an idiot?[162]

185. [163]He may decree that you commit a sin in order to rid you of arrogance and conceit. Indeed, it has been related, "Many a sin is there that causes its perpetrator to enter Paradise."[164] A man offers two units of prayer and relies on them, settles for them, and is delighted by them. This is a good deed surrounded by evil. Another man commits an act of disobedience that brings him a sense of humiliation and brokenness along with unabated humility and poverty of spirit. This is an evil deed surrounded by good.

161. *Shaqrūn*, 37; *N.K.*, 124; *J.K.*, 111: *lā taḥsad illā ʿabdan*, in the active voice. *I.Q.*, 71 has, *lā yuḥsad illā ʿabdun*, in the passive.

162. At this point, *J.K.*, 113 jumps to what I have translated from ¶ 211 all the way up to the end of the first sentence of ¶ 255, except that *J.K.* places what I have in ¶224 where I have ¶225 and what I have in ¶225 where I have ¶224.

163. This is the point to which *J.K.*, 87 had jumped and continued up to line 3 of ¶ 201.

164. *I.Q.*, 71; *rubba dhanbin adkhala ṣāḥibahu al-jannah*; *J.K.*, 87: *dhanb adkhala ṣāḥibahu al-jannah*; *Shaqrūn*, 37; *N.K.*, 125–126 does not cite this report at all. Incidentally, the editors of *I.Q.* (p. 71, nt. 1) indicate that this report appears only in the printed edition(s) on which they relied and that that they were unable to find it in any of the well-known collections of hadith.

186. It is ignorant enough of you that you look to minor transgressions from others while closing your eyes to your own major transgressions.

187. Do not criticize or condemn people according to the apparent dictates of the religious law. Were people today instructed in the ways of the Companions and the Pious Ancestors, they would not be able to handle this. For the latter were God's witnesses against creation.

188. Sin[165] in the sight of those of spiritual insight is like a dead corpse into which dogs poke their noses. Were a man to plunge his mouth into a dead corpse, would you not condemn his action? If God* has commissioned the establishment of scales to regulate buying and selling, will you[166] not establish a scale for measuring the true reality of things?

189. One whose foot is ritually impure is unfit to attend religious gatherings. How much more so is one whose mouth is ritually impure?[167]

190. Whoever acts treacherously will be devalued. Indeed, the legal value of a hand is five hundred gold *dīnār*s. But when it acts treacherously,[168] it is amputated as recompense for stealing the equivalent of a quarter *dīnār*. And whoever has the temerity to commit minor sins will fall into major sins.

191. Know the hidden callings of your self, and do not trust them. If they say to you, "You should visit so and so," you may end

165. *Shaqrūn*, 37; *N.K.*, 128: *J.K.*, 87: *mithāl al-dhanb*; *I.Q.*, 72: *mithāl al-dunyā*.

166. *Shaqrūn*, 38: *fa mā taj'al mīzānan li al-ḥaqā'iq*; *I.Q.*, 72: *a fa mā ja'ala mīzānan li al-ḥaqā'iq*; *N.K.*, 127: *a fa mā taj'al anta mīzānan li al-ḥaqā'iq*; *J.K.*, 88: *a fa mā yaj'al mīzānan li al-ḥaqā'iq*.

167. *N.K.*, 127 adds *bi al-ghībah wa al-namīmah wa qawl al-zūr* (with backbiting, sowing dissension, and false testimony).

168. *I.Q.*, 73; *Shaqrūn*, 38; *N.K.*, 127: *idhā khānat*; *J.K.*, 89: *idhā hanat*.

up going to[169] a raging fire and deliberately casting yourself in. For, this is a time when, in socializing, you rarely sit in a gathering without disobeying God. Thus, many of the Pious Ancestors preferred sitting at home, even to the point of missing congregational prayers. So if your self summons you to leave the house, distract it by sitting at home and engaging in some form of worship.[170] For backbiting in Islam is worse than thirty acts of illicit sex.[171] And dogs go for slumber not to houses with high walls[172] but to garbage dumps.

192. Whoever wants to see examples of the various kinds of hearts, let him look at the various kinds of abodes. Among them are some that are flourishing and peopled;[173] and among them are some that are desolate to the point of becoming outhouses where people go to urinate. Similarly, there is a heart that is like a thriving residence, and a heart that is like a boarded up house.[174] Your sun will not shine until you establish interaction with God.[175] Thus, donate in charity every day, even if but a quarter *dirhām* or a morsel of food, so that God can enter you in the Registry of Donators to Charity. And recite the Qur'ān every day, even if but a verse, so that God can enter you in the Registry of Reciters. Offer supererogatory prayers

169. *I.Q.*, 73; *Shaqrūn*, 38; *N.K.*, 127: *fa rubamā ruḥta*; *J.K.*, 90: *fa rubamā raḥalta*.

170. *N.K.*, 128 adds *ka tilāwat al-qur'ān wa al-ṣalāh wa al-taslīm 'alā al-bashīr al-nadhīr aw tasbīḥ aw istighfār aw ṣalāh nāfilah* (such as reciting the Qur'ān, sending prayers upon the bringer of good tidings and warner (the Prophet) or praising God or asking for forgiveness or supererogatory prayers).

171. The editors of *I.Q.* (p. 73, nt. 2) note that there is a weak hadith to this effect in the book by Ibn Abī al-Dunyā, *Dhamm al-ghībah* (*Condemning Backbiting*), but no such report appears in any of the canonical collections.

172. *I.Q.*, 73–74: *J.K.*, 90: *lā tarqud fī dār 'āliyat al-ḥīṭān*; *Shaqrūn*, 38; *N.K.*, 128: *lā tarqud 'alā al-ḥīṭān*.

173. *N.K.*, 128 omits this line.

174. *Shaqrūn*, 38; *N.K.*, 128; *J.K.*, 90: *wa qalbun ka al-dār al-'āmirah wa qalbun ka al-dār al-kharāb*; *I.Q.*, 74: *wa qalbun ka al-dukkān al-'āmirah wa qalbun ka al-dukkān al-kharāb*.

175. *Shaqrūn*, 38; *N.K.*, 129; *J.K.*, 90: *lā taẓhar shamsuka ḥattā tu'āmila Allāh*; *I.Q.*, 74: *lā taṭhur ḥattā tu'āmila Allāh*.

at night, even if but two units, so that God can register you among the Keepers of Vigils. And do not dare make the mistake of saying, "How can a person who barely has enough provisions for his day-to-day needs donate in charity?" For God* has said, "*Let those of means donate according to their means. And those of limited resources, let them spend according to what God has given them.*"[176] [65:7] Spending on the indigent is like having a pack animal that carries your provisions to the Afterlife.

193. Whoever wants to secure the ultimate things, let him begin by straightening out first things.

194. Whoever is sincere with God, God will protect him from being harmed by enemies[177] and relieve him of having to bear the cost of sustaining supporters. Indeed, whoever is left to rely on the people shall surely debase himself.

195. Do you think that medicine is some kind of sweet you eat? If you do not gallantly force yourself to take it, it will not bring you any cure. Thus, force yourself to repent, and do not be overtaken by the sweetness of disobedience. And when you see your self setting its sights on disobedience, flee to God and seek His aid. He will rescue you.

196. Rather than saying, "Where are the people of initiative; where are the saints; where are the men?" Say, "Where is spiritual insight?" Is one who is smeared in feces[178] fit to see the daughter of the Sultan?

197. On the authority of Shaykh Makīn al-Dīn al-Asmar°: "I was in Alexandria when I saw a sun rise alongside the sun. I marveled at this and drew close to it, when, behold, it was a young man whose

176. *I.Q.*, 74, *Shaqrūn*, 38 and *N.K.*, 129 have this verse. *J.K.*, 90, however, has "*Let him spend of what God has given him.*" [65: 7].

177. *I.Q.*, 75; *Shaqrūn*, 39; *N.K.*, 130: *kafāhu Allāh maḍarrat al-aʿdāʾ wa ḥamala ʿahnu muʾnat al-ardāʾ*. *J.K.*, 91: *kafāhu Allāh wa ḥamala ʿanhu muʾnat al-difāʿ*.

178. *I.Q.*, 75; *Shaqrūn*, 39 *J.K.*, 91: *bi al-ʿadhirah*; *N.K.*, 131: *bi al-qadhar*.

whiskers were just coming in and whose light outshined that of the sun. I greeted him with peace, and he returned my greeting. Then I said to him, 'Where are you from?' He replied, 'I prayed the morning prayer in the Aqsa mosque in Jerusalem. I will offer the noon prayer with you, the afternoon prayer in Mecca and the sunset prayer in Medina.' I said, 'Honor me as a guest.' He said, 'This is not possible.' Then he bade me farewell and left."

198. Whoever honors a believer, it is as if he honors God. And whoever offends a believer, it is as if he offends the latter's Lord and Master. So beware of offending believers. Your self has already taken its fill of evil deeds, and it will be enough for it to carry your weight.

199. Your likeness is that of an onion: once you start peeling it, it turns out to be all peelings.

200. When you want to purify water, you cut off the source of its defilement. Your members are like irrigation channels that flow to the heart. So beware of irrigating your heart with wickedness, such as backbiting, instigation, vile talk, looking at things that are unlawful to look at, and the like. For the heart is veiled not by what comes out of it but by what settles in it. And one brings light into the heart by eating lawful things, remembering God, reciting the Qur'ān, and protecting it from the effects of looking at things that may be permissible, discouraged, or forbidden to look at. Unleash your gaze only on that which is likely to increase your knowledge or wisdom. And rather than saying, "This mirror is dirty," say, "My eyes are inflamed."

201. Love of preeminence, fame, and the like remain with you. Yet you say, "The *shaykh* does not attract our hearts." Say, rather, "The impediment is in me." [179]Had you prepared yourself the first day, you would not need to attend a second session. But, given how

179. At this point, *J.K.*, 93 goes to what I have at ¶140 and continues all the way to the end of ¶ 184. *J.K.*, 133, meanwhile, resumes here.

badly your heart has been tarnished, you need repeated sessions, so that through each one your heart might eventually be polished clean.

202. Turn your affair over to your Lord, and leave those who are incapable of benefiting others. Never mind despairing of the people; direct your hope toward The True King. Look at what He has taught you[180] and at His actions toward you from the beginning of your life. He has shown you nothing but goodness and beneficence. Then look at what you have done. You will see nothing but callousness and disobedience. How often you ally yourself with the people. And how seldom you ally yourself with God.

203. Your members are your flock, your heart is their shepherd,[181] and God is their owner. If you graze your flock in fertile pastures such that their owner is pleased, you will merit his pleasure. But if you graze them in squalid pastures to the point that most of them become emaciated and wolves come and devour some of them, you will merit the owner's punishment. If he wishes, he will retaliate against you; and if he pleases, he will pardon you. Your members[182] are either thus a means to Paradise or a means to Hell. If you direct them toward that which pleases Him, you proceed on the path to Paradise. Otherwise, you proceed on the path to Hell. These are the scales of wisdom. So weigh your intellect on them just like you weigh physical commodities.

204. If you want to know how you are going to pass over the bridge of *Ṣirāṭ*,[183] observe your habit with regard to hastening to

180. *Shaqrūn*, 40: *unẓur mādhā ʿallamaka*; *I.Q.*, 77; *N.K.*, 134: *unẓur mādhā ʿamaluka*. *J.K.*, 133 omits this phrase completely.

181. *I.Q.*, 78; *J.K.*, 134: *wa qalbuka huwa al-rāʿī*; *Shaqrūn*, 40; *N.K.*, 135: *wa anta al-rāʿī* ("and you are their shepherd").

182. *I.Q.*, 78; *J.K.*, 134: *fa jawāriḥuka immā abwāb ilā al-jannah wa immā abwab ilā al-nār*; *Shaqrūn*, 40; *N.K.*, 135: *immā thawāb ilā al-jannah wa immā ʿiqābuka bi al-nār*.

183. A bridge extended over the mouth of Hell over which humans must to pass on the Day of Judgment in order to gain entrance into Paradise.

the mosque. The reward of he who comes to the mosque before the Call to Prayer will be to pass over the bridge of *Ṣirāṭ* like a streak of lightning. And he who comes to the mosque at the beginning of the time for prayer will pass like a prize horse. In this life, however, there is the bridge of uprightness, which cannot be seen with the eye but only with the heart. God* says, "*Verily this is My path, straight, so follow it.*" [6:153] And He merely pointed to the *existence* of this path (not to its physical location). So, for whomever the path is lit, it will be possible for him to follow it. And for whomever the path remains unlit, he will not see it and will remain in a state of confusion. So, if you have for one moment in your life given your ears, eyes, and tongue free reign, now it is time to restrain them.

205. The Prophet* said, "The poor among the believers will enter Paradise before the wealthy by five hundred years."[184] This is because they excelled in this life in worship. You, on the other hand, abandon communal prayers and instead pray alone. And when you do pray, you prostrate like a rooster pecking the earth. But is it proper to present kings with anything other than that which is good and select? The poor only enter Paradise first because they excelled in this life in serving the Master. And by "poor," we mean "steadfast," those who persevere in the face of the bitterness of poverty, to the point that one of them may even rejoice at being afflicted with hardship, just as you rejoice upon finding prosperity. The poor's entering Paradise before the wealthy is thus an indication of their patience[185] in the face of poverty.

184. See Aḥmad b. Ḥanbal, *Musnad al-imām aḥmad b. ḥanbal*, 6 vols. (Beirut: Dār al-Fikr, N.d.), 2: 296, on the authority of Abū Hurayrah.

185. *I.Q.*, 79; *J.K.*, 136: *yadullu 'alā ṣabrihim 'alā al-fāqah*; *Shaqrūn*, 41; *N.K.*, 138: *yadullu 'alā taḥḍīḍihim 'alā al-fāqah*" (is an indication of their having encouraged poverty").

206. It is ignorant enough of you that you frequent the company of people,[186] while turning away from God's door. You engage thereby in all manner of disobedience.[187] Do you not feel sorry for yourself? Indeed, it is the most incredible marvel that a person will commit to a friendship with his self, though evil comes from nowhere but it, while he will refuse a friendship with God, though goodness comes from nowhere but Him.

207. If it is said, "How can one have a friendship with God?" know that the nature of every friendship depends on the thing befriended. Friendship with God* is engendered by fulfilling His commands and honoring his prohibitions. Friendship with the two angels is brought about by giving them good deeds to record. Friendship with the Qur'ān and Sunna is engendered by acting in accordance with their dictates. Friendship with the sky is brought about by reflecting on its wonders. Friendship with the earth is engendered by pondering all the (marvelous) things in it. Now, equality of status is not a precondition of friendship. What is meant by friendship with God is having a proper disposition[188] toward His bounties and favors. One who greets His bounties with gratitude, His trials with patience, His commands with obedience, His prohibitions with restraint, carrying out all his acts of obedience with sincerity—such a person establishes a friendship with God*. And when this friendship becomes firmly entrenched, it turns into mutually intimate fondness.

208. Do not dare say, "Goodness has packed its bags and left." For, we do not need people who cause others to give up on God's

186. *I.Q.*, 79; *N.K.*, 138: *tataraddad ilā al-makhlūq*; *Shaqrūn*, 41: *tataraddad ilā makhlūq*; *J.K.*, 137: *tataraddad ilā bāb al-makhlūq*.

187. *I.Q.*, 80; *Shaqrūn*, 41; *J.K.*, 137: *fa qad irtakabta al-ma'āṣī min kulli jānib*; *N.K.*, 138: *fa in fa'alta dhālika fa qad irtakabta al-ma'āṣī min kulli jānib*.

188. *I.Q.*, 70; *Shaqrūn*, 42; *N.K.*, 139: *ṣuḥbat ayādīhi wa ni'amih*; *J.K.*, 137: *ayādihi wa ni'amih*.

mercy or to despair of Him*. In the Psalms of David, upon him and upon our Prophet be the best of prayers and peace, we read: "I am most merciful to My servant when he turns away from Me." Indeed, many an obedient person perishes, due to his conceit. And many a sinner is forgiven, due to his broken heartedness.

209. On the authority of Shaykh Makīn al-Dīn al-Asmar: "I saw a slave with his master in Alexandria, the two of them dwarfed by a flag that filled the distance between heaven and earth. I said, 'I wonder if this flag belongs to the master or the slave.' I followed them until the master bought something for the slave and the latter departed. When the slave left, the flag left with him. I knew, then, that he was one of God's* saints. So, I approached the master and said, 'Will you sell me this slave?' He said, 'Why?' And he continued to question me until I mentioned to him what I had seen. He said to me, 'Sir, I am more likely to provide you with what you are looking for.' Then he proceeded to free the slave, he being a great saint."

210. There are those who know the saints by smell, even in the absence of perfume. And there are those who know them by taste: when they see a saint, they get a good taste in their mouths; and when they see someone who is disconnected, they get a bitter taste in their mouths.[189]

211. [190]One who does not abandon forbidden things will not benefit from carrying out obligatory acts: one who does not take preventative measures[191] will not benefit from medicine.

212. How diminished the blessing of plundered money is. This, by God, is the life of the heedless—plundered!

189. *J.K.*, 139 ends here and the text jumps to what I have at ¶255. In fact, the first line of ¶ 255 is repeated at *J.K.*, 132–133 and 139.

190. *J.K.*, 113 resumes here.

191. *I.Q.*, 81; *Shaqrūn*, 43; *N.K.*, 141: *man lam yaḥtami*; *J.K.*, 113: *wa man lam yanfaʿhu al-dawāʾ lam yazal ʿindahu al-dāʾ wa man lam yaḥtami lam yanfaʿhu al-dawāʾ*.

213. The life of this world is like a leprous, psoriatic old hag covered in silk clothing. The believer is repulsed by her and turns others away from her, because her true nature is exposed to him. And no one wears a more putrid uniform than that of pretentiousness, whereby one says during a disputation, "And you are my equal?" "And you are fit to address me?" "And who are you that I should address you?" The first one to perish for this was Iblīs. So beware of this. And this applies even if your adversary is a crippled, mangy, leper. Do not look upon him with contempt; for the existence of "There is no god but God" in his heart makes him inviolable. Think well of everyone, you will prosper.

214. Do you think that good character is simply for a person to be pleasant? One who honors people but tramples up on the rights of God* does not have good character. Rather, a person is not credited with good character until he recognizes God's* rights, observes His rules, fulfills His commands, and honors His prohibitions. And whoever forbids himself from disobeying God and fulfills his obligations to God is a person of good character.

215. God has only unleashed the people's tongues against you so that you can return to Him. Do you not see that as long as you do not disobey God you have value with Him, but when you disobey Him, you have no value? God-consciousness is abstaining from disobedience to God, even where no one sees you.

216. When the Prophet* drank water he would say, "Praise be to God who made this sweet and fresh by His mercy and did not make it salty and bitter because of our sins."[192] Now, the Prophet* was purified of sin, but he said this out of humility and in order to instruct us. He could have said, "Because of *your* sins." But he only ate and

192. At *I.Q.*, 73, nt. 1, the editors report that al-Ṭabarānī and al-Hindī relate such a report in *Kanz al-ʿummāl*, no. 18226, without indicating its degree of soundness.

drank in the manner he did in order to teach us proper etiquette. Otherwise, he used to receive food and drink directly from God. Thus, those of supersensory knowledge bow their heads when they drink, and tears may even trickle from their eyes, as they say, "This is a manifestation of God's* love."

217. Some of them refused to attend communal prayers because of the molestations they used to encounter along the way. Among them was Mālik b. Anas°. This is because they understood that the communal aspect of prayer constitutes profit that is only computed after the capital expenditures have been covered.[193]

218. Do not think[194] that predatory animals reside in the open country. Predatory animals reside in the markets and thoroughfares. They are the ones who viciously maul people's hearts.

219 One who continually sins and asks for forgiveness is like one who continually drinks poison and follows it up with the antidote. It should be said to this person, "You may not make it to the antidote one day, and death may overtake you before you are able to administer it."

220. One whose heart is diseased will be prevented from wearing the garb of God-consciousness. Were your heart free of the diseases of undisciplined passion and unwarranted carnal desire, you would be able to bear the burdens of God-consciousness. One's failure to find sweetness in obedience is an indication that one's heart is diseased with carnal desire. Indeed, God* has called carnal desire a disease when He said, ". . . *lest he in whose heart lies a disease should desire. . . .*" [33: 32] Now, there are two ways by which you must treat this: 1) partaking of what is good for you, namely obedience; and

193. *I.Q.*, 73; *Shaqrūn*, 44; *N.K.*, 144–145: *wa al-ribḥ lā yuḥsab illā ba'da al-iḥātah 'alā ra's al-māl*; *J.K.*, 115: *wa al-ribḥ ba'da ra's al-māl lā yajib*.

194. *I.Q.*, 83: *lā taḥsab al-sibā'*; *Shaqrūn*, 44; *N.K.*, 145; *J.K.*, 115: *laysa al-sibā'*.

2) avoiding what is harmful to you, namely disobedience. If you commit a sinful act but follow it by repentance, remorsefulness, broken-spiritedness, and contrition, this will be a cause via which you reconnect with Him. And if you perform an act of obedience but follow it by conceit and arrogance, this will be a cause via which you are disconnected from Him.

221. How strange it is[195] that you seek to restore your heart while your members partake as they please of forbidden things,[196] such as unlawful gazes, backbiting, sowing dissension, and other such things. In this regard, you are like a person who takes poison for medicine or one who wants to clean his clothing with soot. You should take to solitude and isolation. For one who takes isolation as his habit will find honor as his companion. And one who is sincere in his isolation, will find God's complimentary gifts bounteously bestowed. The signs of this are the removal of the covering, the revivification of the heart, and the realization of love. So, perform good deeds, not simply numerous ones. For performing numerous deeds that are not good is like wearing numerous sets of cheap clothing. And performing few deeds that are good is like wearing few sets of expensive clothing—like an emerald, small in size but great in value. Thus, one who occupies his heart with God and fortifies it against the assaults of undisciplined passions is better than one who simply engages in much prayer and fasting.

222. One who offers a prayer in which his heart is not present is like one who gifts a king a hundred (gift-wrapped) empty boxes. Such a person deserves to be punished by this king.[197] One who

195. *N.K.*, 146 adds *yā hādhā* (good sir).

196. *I.Q.*, 84; *Shaqrūn*, 44; *J.K.*, 146: *min al-muḥarramāt*; *J.K.*, 116: *min al-mukhālafāt al-muḥarramāt.*

197. *N.K.*, 148 adds *yadhkuruhu 'alayhā dā'iman* (he will remember him forever for this).

offers a prayer in which his heart is present is like one who gifts a king an emerald worth a thousand gold *dīnārs*. This king will remember him forever for this.

223. When you enter into prayer, you enter a private conversation with God*, and you talk to the Prophet*. For you say, "Peace be unto you, O Prophet, along with God's mercy and blessings." And the Arabs only use the vocative, "*ayyuhā*," followed by a definite noun to address persons directly.

224. Two units of supererogatory prayer at night are better than a thousand during the day. And you only offer such prayers to find them[198] in the scale that weighs your deeds. Does anyone purchase a slave except for the services the latter performs? Have you seen anyone purchase a slave merely so that the latter can eat and sleep? You are simply a slave who has been purchased. God* said, "*Verily God has purchased from the believers their souls and possessions in exchange for Paradise. They fight in the path of God wherein they kill and are killed.*" [9: 111][199]

225. Anyone who does not place obligations on his self will find the latter clinging to him. And anyone who does not make demands of his self will find that it makes demands of him. Were you to place upon your self the burdens of obedience, it would not demand disobedient action of you, nor would it have time to do so. Do you see the righteous and devout aimlessly cruising at Eid celebrations? Whoever busies himself with even lawful indulgences and amusement will be distracted from night vigils. It will be said to them, "You distracted yourself away from Us, so We distracted you away from worshipping Us."

198. *I.Q.*, 85; *Shaqrūn*, 45; *N.K.*, 148: *lā tuṣalli rakʿatayn illā li tajida dhālika*; *J.K.*, 118: *lā tuṣalli rakʿatayn fa tajida dhālika*.

199. *N.K.*, 149 cites the verse in full.

226. Two units of prayer in the dead of night weigh more heavily upon you than the mountain of Uḥud. But members that have become too rigid for worship are only fit for amputation. Like trees, when they dry up they become fit for nothing but fire.

227. One whose heart is attached to the life of this world is like one who builds a beautiful structure over which sits a toilet that leaks down on it. Such a person will continue in this state until his outer appearance comes to reflect his inner reality. There are people, however, who cleanse their hearts, as a result of which their hearts remain pure. And cleansing the heart is by repentance, remembrance, remorsefulness, and asking for forgiveness. Here you are, though (like this leaked-on, beautiful structure) in the presence of God, soiled with disobedience, partaking of forbidden things and gazes. And one who engages in such violations and indulges his carnal desires merely darkens his own heart. If you do not repent while you are healthy, He may test you with sickness and tribulations, that you may emerge cleansed of sin, like a garment when it is washed. So cleanse the mirror of your heart through solitude and remembrance of God until you meet God*. And let your remembrance be a single refrain,[200] that divinely sponsored illuminations may spring forth for you. Do not be like a person who wants to dig a well but merely digs a foot here and a foot there, as a result of which water never springs forth for him. Dig in one place, that water may spring forth for you.

228. O servant of God, your religion is your capital. If you squander your religion, you squander your capital.[201] Let your tongue be busied with remembrance of Him, your heart with love of Him, and

200. *I.Q.*, 87: *wa'l yakun dhikran wāḥidan*; *Shaqrūn*, 46; *J.K.*, 151: *wa'l yakun qalbuka dhākiran* (and let your heart be filled with remembrance).

201. *I.Q.*, 87; *Shaqrūn*, 46: *fa in ḍayya'tahu ḍayya'ta ra's mālik*. *N.K.*, 152: *fa in ḍayya'ta ra's mālika fa'shghal lisānak bi al-dhikr*. This line is missing from *J.K.*, 121.

your members with serving Him. Cultivate your existence with the proper tools,[202] that the seeds you sow may bring forth produce. And whoever does with his heart as the farmers do with their fields will enlighten his heart.

229. Your likeness is that of two men each of whom buys a plot of land of the same dimensions. One of them takes this land, clears it of thorns and wild grass, irrigates it, and plants it. It yields crops, he harvests these and benefits from them. This is the likeness of one reared in obedience. The lights of his heart shine forth. As for the other man, he ignores his plot to the point that thorns and wild grass grow in it and it becomes a sanctuary for vipers and snakes. This person's heart has been darkened by disobedience.

230. [203]If you attend religious gatherings and then go right out and fall into violations and heedless indulgences, do not dare say, "What good does it do me to attend?" Rather, attend! [204]Your sickness has been with you for forty years. Do you expect it to disappear in a single hour or a single day? Your likeness is that of sand[205] thrown into a single spot for forty years. Do you expect it to be removed in a single hour or a single day? Even were he to plunge himself into seven seas, he who has persisted in disobedience and wallowed in forbidden acts would not be cleansed until he first enters into a pact of repentance with God.

231. There is a major ritual impurity that afflicts the outward person and prohibits him from entering His House or reciting His Book.[206] And there is a major ritual impurity that afflicts the inner person and prohibits him from entering His presence or understanding

202. *I.Q.*, 87; *Shaqrūn*, 46; *N.K.*, 152: *bi al-maḥārith*; *J.K.*, 121: *bi al-makhāwif.*
203. *N.K.*, 152 adds *yā hādhā* (good sir).
204. *N.K.*, 153 adds the interrogative "*a*" here.
205. *I.Q.*, 88; *Shaqrūn*, 47; *N.K.*, 153: *ka raml*; *J.K.*, 122: *ka zibl.*
206. *I.Q.*, 88; *Shaqrūn*, 47; *N.K.*, 153: *tilāwat kitābih*; *J.K.*, 123: *tilāwat kalāmih.*

His words. This is heedlessness. Whenever your self petitions you to satisfy some carnal desire, bridle it with the religious law. For it is like a pack animal inclining toward a neighbor's crops. Divert[207] your eyes away from inclining toward worldly vanities and your heart away from inclining toward unwarranted carnal pleasures. And let your heart be always enlivened and thus unfit for such things.[208] For God* chooses to take into His company those who are fit.[209] And those who are not fit He consigns to created beings. These two groups are like slaves who are presented to a king: those the king takes into his service are honored; the rest are left to the common plight of slaves.

232. Anytime you come into a circle of wisdom or a circle of disobedience you will carry around your neck a chain of light or darkness. If you yourself are unable to see this chain, others are able to see it. Do you not see that the entire population sees the sun except for the blind?

233. What is the point of knowledge except action in accordance with it? Its likeness is that of a king who writes instructions to his governor at the border of the empire. What is the point of these instructions: for him simply to read them? The point is for him to act in accordance with them.

234. The likeness of one who seeks knowledge while lacking insight is that of a hundred thousand blind persons stumbling along a path. Were there to appear among them a single person with even a single eye, people would all follow him and leave the hundred thousand blind people.

207. *I.Q.*, 88; *J.K.*, 123: *fa ghuḍḍa; Shaqrūn*, 47; *N.K.*, 154: *fa ghammiḍ.*

208. *Shaqrūn*, 47: *wa'l yakun qalbuka ma'mūran lā yaṣluḥ lahā 'alā al-dawām*; *I.Q.*, 88: *wa'l yakun qalbuka ma'mūran 'alā al-dawām*; *J.K.*, 123: *wa'l yakun qalbuka ma'mūran bi dhikr Allāh 'alā al-dawām*; *N.K.*, 154: *wa'l yakun qalbuka ma'mūran bi al-taqwā 'alā al-dawām.*

209. *N.K.*, 154 has *wa al-ḥaqq lā yakhtāru li ḥaḍratihi illā man ṣalaḥa lahā* (God only takes into His presence those who are fit).

235. A scholar[210] who does not live by the knowledge he has is like a candle[211] that leads the way for others by burning itself out. Even ignorance is better than knowledge shot through with heedlessness of God.

236. One whose members bear fruit has a heart that irrigates his tongue[212] with remembrance of God, his eyes with being closed to worldly temptations, his ears with listening to knowledge, and his hands and feet with going forth in pursuit of good.

237. Whoever frequents the company of the people of our time exposes himself to disobeying God*. Such a person is like one who places dry firewood into a fire and hopes that it will not ignite. They hope for the impossible, for it has all but occurred.

238. To be popular among the people is to be singled out for affliction. One who knows the people, however, and lives among them is not like one who does not know them.[213] For, while you may be God-conscious, you may fall into the company of people who are not, as a result of which they draw you into backbiting and subjugate your spirit.

239. Nothing destroys hearts but the paucity of fear.[214]

240. The good heart is the one that is not distracted from God* by good things. If you want to heal your heart, repair to the desert of repentance, convert your spiritual state from absence to presence,[215]

210. *I.Q.*, 89: *al-ʿālim*; *Shaqrūn*, 48; *J.K.*, 124; *N.K.*, 155: *al-ʿilm* (knowledge).

211. *N.K.*, 155 adds *al-mūqadah* (lighted [candle]).

212. *I.Q.*, 90; *N.K.*, 155: *fa qad amṭara qalbuhu lisānahu bi al-dhikr*; *Shaqrūn*, 48: *amṭara qalbahu wa lisānahu al-dhikr*; *J.K.*, 125: *amṭara qalbahu wa lisānahu bi al-dhikr*.

213. *I.Q.*, 90; *Shaqrūn*, 48 and *J.K.*, 125 all give *wa ʿāsha fīhim man lam yaʿrifhum* (And not to know them is to be able to live among them). *N.K.*, 157 gives *khuṣṣa al-balāʾ bi man ʿarafa al-nās wa ʿāsha fīhim man lam yaʿrifhum*. *I.Q.*, 90, nt 3, however, indicates that the manuscript on which they relied gives *man arafa al-nās wa ʿāsha fīhim laysa ka man lam yaʿrifhum*. I have chosen to go with this.

214. *N.K.*, 157 adds *min al-mawlā al-karīm* (of the Generous Master).

215. *J.K.*, 126 adds *wa al-ḥaḍrah*.

and don the robe of humility and meekness. For hearts can be healed. But you stuff your belly and then boast about being fat. You are like a lamb that is fattened for slaughter. Indeed, have you not slaughtered your self, while you are unaware?

241. Do not allow yourself to miss a session of wisdom, even if you remain in a state of disobedience. And do not say, "What is the point of listening to these sessions, while I remain unable to desist from disobedience?" The archer must continue to shoot! If he does not take home game today, he will take it tomorrow.[216]

242. Were you clever and smart, God's rights would take precedence over the fortunes of your self. Only trustworthy persons are granted access to secrets. But you grant your self its allotment of food and drink only to fill your toilet. Is it not enough that you love the life of this world?[217] For loving the life of this world is an act of treachery. Do kings grant treacherous persons access to their secrets? Use your supplications, and rely on Him to send down illuminations.[218]

243. Nothing benefits the heart like isolating oneself and entering the arena of self-scrutiny. How can a heart radiate light when images of created beings are stamped onto its mirror? How can one make one's way to God while one remains prostrate[219] to one's carnal desires? How can one aspire to enter the presence of God while one has yet to purify oneself of the major impurity of heedlessness? And how can one hope to understand the subtleties of the inner secrets while one has yet to repent of one's lapses?

216. According to *I.Q.*, 90, nt. 1, from "Do not allow" all the way to "tomorrow" does not appear in their manuscript. *Shaqrūn*, 48, *N.K.*, 158 and *J.K.*, 126, however, all include this segment as translated here.

217. *J.K.*, 127; *N.K.*, 159: *wa yakfīka*; *I.Q.*, 91; *Shaqrūn*, 49: *a wa yakfīka*.

218. *I.Q.*, 91; *N.K.*, 159: *J.K.*, 127: *wa 'alayhi inzāl al-anwār*. *I.Q.*, 91, nt. 3, indicates that this last sentence does not appear in the printed edition on which the editors relied. *Shaqrūn*, 49, however, gives: *fa'sta'mil al-afkār wa 'alayhi anzala al-anwār*.

219. *I.Q.*, 91; *Shaqrūn*, 49; *N.K.*, 159: *munkabb*; *J.K.*, 127: *mukabbal*, "shackled to."

244. The source of every instance of disobedience, heedlessness, and surrender to carnal passion[220] is being pleased with one's self. And the source of every instance of obedience, awareness, and abstemiousness is a lack of being pleased with one's self.

245. Do not pass from created reality to created reality, as if you were a donkey rotating around a millstone. He walks, and the very thing from which he passes is the thing to which he passes. Rather, pass from created reality to the Creator: "*Verily, your Lord is the terminus ad quem.*" [53: 42]

246. Illumination is simply the pack animal of the heart and inner conscience. Indeed, light is the soldier of the heart, as darkness is the soldier of the self. Thus, when God wants to assist[221] His servant, He provides him with soldiers of illumination and cuts off the supply of darknesses and alternate centers of attention. Light has the function of disclosure. Inner vision has the function of discernment. And the heart has the function of advancing or turning away.

247. The outward appearance of created things promotes deception. The inner reality of created things warns of lessons to be learned. The self looks to the deceptive properties of outward appearances. The heart looks to lessons to be learned from inner realities. Whenever God causes you to feel alienated from His creatures, know that He simply wants to open for you a door to intimacy with Him.

248. Prayer is an occasion of private communication and a repository of goodwill. During it, the province of one's inner conscience expands and brilliant illuminations radiate. He knew, however, of the presence of weakness in you; thus He limited the

220. *J.K.*, 128: *N.K.*, 159: *ma'ṣīyah wa ghaflah wa shahwah*; *I.Q.*, 92; *Shaqrūn*, 49: *ma'ṣīyah wa ghaflah wa sahw*.

221. *I.Q.*, 92: *Shaqrūn*, 49; *N.K.*, 160: *yanṣur*; *J.K.*, 129: *yu'izz*.

number of required prayers. But He also knew of your need for His grace; thus He made plentiful the benefits of prayer.

249. People praise you for what they *think* of you. You, however, should rebuke yourself for what you *know* of you. Indeed, the most ignorant people are those who ignore what they know with certainty in exchange for what the people merely think. Shut out the influence of people's gazing at you through your knowledge of God's gazing at you. And be oblivious to their advances through witnessing His.

250. He knows that people aspire to uncover the secrets of His hidden providence. He* said, "*He singles out for His mercy whomsoever He wills.*[222] *And God is possessed of mighty grace.*" [2: 105] But He knows[223] that had He allowed them easy access to this, they would abandon action, relying instead on what had been sempiternally decreed. Thus, says God*, "*Verily, God's mercy is near to the doers of good.*" [7: 56] If you want complimentary divine gifts to come to you, confirm your commitment to poverty and need: "*Charity is simply for the poor and needy.*" [9: 60]

251. There are divinely sponsored illuminations that have been authorized to enter and divinely sponsored illuminations that have been authorized to connect. And it may happen that illuminations come to you but find your heart filled with vestiges of unsavory influences and thus depart whence they descended. Empty your heart of all others, and He will fill it with supersensory knowledge and hidden secrets.

252. The believer is too preoccupied with extolling God to applaud himself. And he is too preoccupied with the rights of God to remember his own fortunes.

222. *J.K.*, 130 has only the first part of this verse.
223. *N.K.*, 162: *wa''lam.*

253. God has placed you in the intermediate world, between His earthly and heavenly kingdoms, in order to show you your exalted status among His creatures and that you are a precious gem whose outer make-up is merely a casing.[224] You exist with created realities as long as you do not witness the Creator. But when you witness the Creator, created realities come to exist with you.

254. The reasonable person is happier with that which is lasting than he is with that which fades. His inner light radiates and his prescience comes forth. Thus, he turns away from this abode and leaves it behind,[225] forsaking it and closing his eyes to it, neither taking it as a home nor making it a resting place. Rather, he hefts his spiritual ambition away from it toward God*, repairing to Him and seeking His assistance in reaching Him, his mount of determination never wavering but, rather, complying with his spiritual ambition[226] to the point that it is brought to kneel at the precinct of holiness and the carpet of intimacy, the place of disclosure and mutual encounter, of direct interaction and communion, of actual seeing and benignity. Divine presence comes, thus, to fill their hearts and they seek refuge in it and take it as their home. If they descend to the heaven of rights and the earth of worldly fortunes, this is by God's permission[227] and empowerment and by their being firmly grounded in certainty. Thus, they do not descend to rights through bad etiquette and heedlessness nor to worldly fortunes on the basis of carnal desire and simple enjoyment. Rather, they enter all of this by God, for God, from God, and to God.[228]

224. *I.Q.*, 94; *Shaqrūn*, 50; *N.K.*, 164: *aṣdāf mukawwanātih*; *J.K.*, 131: *asdāf maknūnātih*.

225. *I.Q.*, 94: *wa a'raḍa 'anhā mughḍīyan*; *J.K.*, 132; *Shaqrūn*, 50; *N.K.*, 165: *wa a'raḍa 'anhā mughḍiban*.

226. *Shaqrūn*, 50; *N.K.*, 165: *tusāyiruhā*; *I.Q.*, 94: *tasāyuruhā*; *J.K.*, 132: *bi tasyārihā*.

227. *I.Q.*, 95; *Shaqrūn*, 51: *fa bi al-idhn*; *J.K.*, 132: *fa bi al-idhlāl*.

228. *J.K.* stops here and begins with first sentence of what I have at ¶ 255. According to *I.Q.*, 95, nt. 3, from what I have at ¶241, i.e., "Nothing benefits the heart . . ." all the way up to the end of ¶ 254 does not appear in the manuscript on which they relied. All of this appears,

255. [229]Thus, beware, my brother, of listening to those who criticize this party, lest you be diminished in the sight of God and evoke His disgust.[230] For these people have sat before God in true honesty and pure integrity,[231] scrutinizing their every breath before God. They have surrendered their reigns to Him and voluntarily cast their souls before Him, abandoning attempts to gain victory for their selves, out of a sense of shame before their Lord. Thus, He came to be the One to fight in their behalf against anyone who fights against them. And He came to be the One who will overtake anyone who seeks to overtake them.

256. Now, God has tested this party with certain people, especially scholars.[232] Indeed, you will rarely find a scholar whose breast God has expanded to the point that he believes in any individual saint. Rather, he will say to you, "Yes, saints exist, but where are they?" Then, no one will be mentioned to him without his denying any special relationship between this person and God, unleashing his tongue with all manners of argumentation, bereft of any belief in this person's sainthood. Beware of people who are like this. And flee from them as you would a lion!

257. Shaykh Abū al-Ḥasan (al-Shādhilī)° said, "The jurist is not the one the eyes of whose heart the veil has rendered inoperable.[233] The jurist is simply one who understands the secret of creation and that God only brought him into existence for the purpose of worshipping Him and that He only created him for the purpose of

however, in *Shaqrūn*, 49–51, *N.K.*, 158–156, and *J.K.*, 126–133. *I.Q.* apparently relied either on *Shaqrūn* or another printed edition.

229. *J.K.*, 139, last paragraph starts here.

230. *J.K.*, 133 stops here and jumps to what I have at ¶ 201.

231. *I.Q.*, 95; *Shaqrūn*, 51; *N.K.*, 166: *wa ikhlāṣ al-wafā'*; *J.K.*, 140: *wa al-ikhlāṣ wa al-wafā'*.

232. *I.Q.*, 96; *Shaqrūn*, 51; *N.K.*, 167: *ahl al-'ilm*; *J.K.*, 140: *ahl al-'ilm al-ẓāhir*.

233. *I.Q.*, 96; *Shaqrūn*, 51; *N.K.*, 167: *faqa'a al-ḥijāb 'aynay qalbih*; *J.K.*, 141: *faqa'a al-ḥijāb 'an 'aynay qalbih*.

serving Him. If he understands this, this knowledge of his will be a cause for him to abstain from the vanities of this world and devote himself to the Afterlife, ignoring the fortunes of his self and working to fulfill the rights of his Master, thinking about the resurrection and preparing for it."

258. The Prophet* said, "The strong believer is better in the sight of God than the weak. But in both of them is good."[234] The strong believer is the one in whose heart the light of certainty radiates.

259. God* said, "*The Forerunners, the Forerunners, they are the ones who will be brought close. In gardens of delight.* [56: 10–12] They led the way to God, so He[235] purified their hearts of everything besides Him, such that no impediments impeded them and no worldly attachments distracted them. Thus, they led the way to God, since there was nothing to prevent them from doing so.

260. Indeed, people are only prevented from leading the way to God by the pull of attachments to things other than God. Every time their hearts aspire to betake to God*, these attachments pull them away. Their hearts then turn back toward these attachments and pursue them. Coming into the divine presence is thus forbidden to such people and denied to those so characterized. This is the context in which you should understand His* statement, "*On the day when neither wealth nor progeny will avail anyone; (no one will benefit) save those who come to God with a pure heart.*" [26: 88–89] The pure heart is one that is not attached to anything but God*. Then there is His* statement, "*You have now come to Us as individuals as We created you in the beginning. And now you have left behind all that We granted you in this life.*" [6: 94] From this it is understood that you will not be

234. See *Ṣaḥīḥ muslim*, 4: 1629: "The strong believer is better and more beloved to God than the weak believer. But in both of them is good. . . ."

235. *Shaqrūn*, 52; *J.K.*, 141–142; *N.K.*, 168: *fa khallaṣa qulūbahum*; *I.Q.*, 97: *fa khallaṣū qulūbahum*.

fit to come to God nor to arrive in His presence unless you are detached from all others besides Him. And from His* statement, "*Did He not find you an orphan and shelter you?*" [93: 6] you should understand that God will not shelter you unless your status as an orphan to everyone except Him is confirmed. And the Prophet's* statement, "God is odd in number and loves numerical oddness,"[236] means that He loves the heart that is not attached to dual influences. Such hearts are for God and by God. And these are the people of divine presence, who are addressed through divine benevolence. How could they rely upon other than Him when they are direct witnesses to the reality of His Oneness?

261. Shaykh Abū al-Ḥasan al-Shādhilī° said: "Direct witnessing became too intense for me,[237] so I asked Him to shield me from it. It was said to me, 'Even were you to ask in the name of what Moses, His direct communicant, Jesus, His spirit, or Muhammad*, His beloved, intimate, asked, He would not grant you this. Rather, ask Him to make you strong enough to bear it.' So I asked, and He strengthened me."

262. People of understanding take from God[238] (directly) and place their trust in Him. They are able to subsist, thus, on His aid, and He relieves them of their concerns and turns away from them that which would cause them grief. They distract themselves with what He has commanded them away from any preoccupation with what He has taken upon Himself to guarantee, knowing that He will neither consign them to any other nor deny them His favor. Thus, they enter a state of rest, basking in the garden of submission and the delight of delegating their affair to God. God thus raises their stature and perfects their light.

236. *Ṣaḥīḥ muslim*, 4: 1638.

237. *J.K.*, 144 adds *marratan* (once).

238. *I.Q.*, 98; *Shaqrūn*, 53; *N.K.*, 171: *ahl al-fahm akhadhū ʿan Allāh wa tawakkalū ʿalayh*; *J.K.*, 144: *ahl al-fahm ʿan Allāh tawakkalū ʿalayh.*

263. Know, may God* have mercy on you, that wherever "knowledge" is repeated in the Mighty Book or purified Sunna, this is a reference to beneficial knowledge that is accompanied by godly fear and surrounded by trepidation. God* said, "*Verily, it is the knowledgeable among God's servants who fear Him.*" [35: 28] Thus, He made it clear that knowledge is invariably accompanied by godly fear. The knowledgeable, therefore, are the people of godly fear. Likewise, He* said, "*Verily those who were given knowledge before this . . .*," [17: 107] and "*Those firmly grounded in knowledge,*" [4: 162] and, "*Say, Lord increase me in knowledge.*" [20: 114] And the Prophet* said, "The scholars are the heirs of the Prophets."[239] In all of these places, "knowledge" simply refers to beneficial knowledge that overpowers undisciplined passions and subdues the self. This is necessarily the meaning here, because the speech of God* and His Messenger* is too lofty to be interpreted any other way. Beneficial knowledge is that which aids us in remaining obedient and inspires fear of God* and dutiful observation of His* limits. It is, in a word, knowledge grounded in supersensory knowledge of God*.

264. But, those who carelessly espouse monotheism (*tawḥīd*) without observing the plain dictates of *sharīʿah* are cast into the sea of crypto-infidelity (*zandaqah*).[240] Indeed, the important thing is to be supported by the inner truth (*ḥaqīqah*) while binding oneself by the dictates of *sharīʿah*. This is the way of the spiritual masters: they neither bolt forth, limiting themselves to the inner truth, nor stop short, limiting themselves to apparent attributions to *sharīʿah*. Rather, they follow a position between these two extremes. To stop short and limit oneself to apparent attributions to *sharīʿah* is to

239. See *Sunan abī dāʾūd*, 2:407

240. For a discussion on the meaning of "*zandaqah*," see my *On the Boundaries of Theological Tolerance in Islam: Abū Ḥāmid al-Ghazālī's Fayṣal al-Tafriqa* (New York: Oxford University Press, 2002), 55–59.

associate divinity with other than God (*shirk*). To bolt forth with the inner truth without binding oneself to the dictates of *sharīʿah* is to subvert the Faith. Guidance is the middle path.

265. Any bit of knowledge that springs to your mind carrying disquieting notions followed by images to which your self inclines and in which your nature delights, throw it away, even if it is true. Avail yourself of the knowledge of God that He revealed to the Messenger of God*. And follow the example of the Messenger, the Caliphs after him, and the Companions and Successors after them, along with those who guide people to God*, the great Imams who are absolved of undisciplined passion, and their followers[241]; you will be spared doubts, suppositions, erroneous impressions, whisperings, and false claims that mislead away from guidance and its realities. Ultimately, knowledge of God's oneness is all the beneficial knowledge you need.

266. It is a form of knowledge[242] to love God, His Messenger*, and the Companions, as well as believing that the Community is a repository of truth. But if you want to have a share of what God's* saints have, you must reject the generality of the people, save those who show you the way to God*, either through their authentic, non-verbal, intimations or by their well-established deeds, which are contradicted neither by the Qur'ān nor the Sunna. Raise your ambition toward your Master, and busy yourself with Him to the exclusion of all besides Him. I heard Shaykh Abū al-ʿAbbās al-Mursī say, "By God, I have seen honor in nothing save raising one's ambition above being preoccupied with the people."

241. *Shaqrūn*, 54: *wa mutābiʿīhim*; *I.Q.*, 101: *wa mutābaʿatihim*; *N.K.*, 175: *wa mutābaʿatuhum tusallim*; *J.K.*, 148: *wa bi mutābaʿtihim.*

242. While all editions give *wa min al-ʿilm*, *I.Q.*, 101, nt. 1 indicates that the manuscript has *wa min al-ʿamal*, which would obviously change the point of this segment.

267. Remember His* statement here, may God have mercy on you: "*To God belongs honor, and to His Prophet and the believers.*" [63: 8] And part of the honor that God confers upon the believer is the believer's raising his ambitions toward his Master and having ultimate trust in Him, to the exclusion of all besides Him.

268. Have some shame before God, lest, after He has clothed you in the garb of faith and adorned you with the ornament of accurate perception, heedlessness and forgetfulness should overtake you to the point that you incline toward created entities or seek benevolence from other than Him.

269. Foul it is of a believer that he should present his needs to other than his Master, despite his knowledge of His oneness and exclusive Lordship, having heard God's* statement, "*Is not God sufficient for His servants.*" [39: 36] And he should remember God's* statement, "*O you who believe, honor your commitments.*" [5: 1] And among the commitments you have made is that you not ultimately present your needs to anyone but Him and that you not place your ultimate trust in anyone but Him. Raising your ambition above preoccupation with the people is the true measure of humility.[243] "*Set up the scales justly.*" [55: 9]

270. The truthful will be known by their truthfulness and the false claimers by their lies. In His wisdom and benevolence, God has tried those who feign humility by exposing the urges they conceal and the carnal desires they keep secret, whereby they degrade themselves before worldly people, embracing the latter with open arms and complying with their every wish, yet being rejected at their doorsteps.[244] You will see one of them dressed to the nines

243. *I.Q., mīzān al-faqr; Shaqrūn*, 55; *N.K.*, 178; *J.K.*, 149: *mīzān al-fuqarā'*.

244. *I.Q.*, 102: *Shaqrūn*, 55; *N.K.*, 179: *madfū'īn 'an abwābihim; J.K.*, 150: *madfū'īn 'alā abwābihim*.

like a bride, taking a keen interest[245] in primping his outward appearance, ignoring all the while the need to reform his inner being. God has branded such a person in a manner that exposes his depravities and discloses his affair. Thus, after his affiliation with God had earned him—had he been sincere—the name, "servant of The Grand" (*'Abd al-Kabīr*), he is removed from this affiliation and called "the governor's pet" (*shaykh al-amīr*). Such people invent lies against God* and impede others from establishing a relationship with God's saints. For the common people take everything they see in these people and attribute it to those who affiliate themselves with God, sincerely or insincerely. Thus, these people are veils upon the People of True Realization and rain clouds around the sun of the People of Facilitation. They beat their drums, raise their flags, and don their armor. But when the battle begins, they turn on their heels and shrink in retreat. Their tongues flap with pretentious claims, while their hearts are devoid of God-consciousness. Have they not heard His* statement, "*That He may question the truthful about their truthfulness*"? [33: 8] If He is going to question the truthful about their truthfulness, shall those who make pretentious claims be left without being questioned? Have they not heard His* statement, "*Say, work, God will see your deeds, as will His Messenger and the believers. And you will be returned to the Knower of the unseen and the seen, and He will inform you of what you used to do*"? [9: 105] They make show in the garb of the truthful,[246] while their deeds are the deeds of those who turn their backs on service to God.[247]

245. *I.Q.*, 102; *Shaqrūn*, 55; *N.K.*, 179: *mu'tanūn bi iṣlāḥ ẓahwāhirim*; *J.K.*, 150: *maftūnūn bi iṣlāḥ ẓawāhirihim.*

246. *J.K.*, adds *ṣāliḥīn* ("righteous") before "truthful."

247. *I.Q.*, 103; *Shaqrūn*, 56; *J.K.*, 180: *wa 'amaluhum 'amal al-mu'riḍīn*; *J.K.*, 151: *wa 'amaluhum ghayr 'amal al-mu'minīn.*

271. God* said, "*Enter homes through their doors.*" [2: 189] Know that the door to provision is obedience to The Provider. How, then, can things be requested of Him through disobedience? Or how can one seek to have His bounties rain down on him through violating His commands? The Prophet, upon him be the best prayers and peace, said, "What God has cannot be gained by displeasing Him."[248] That is to say, His provisions can only be sought through pleasing Him.[249] God* said, clarifying this point, "*Whoever is conscious of God, He will make a way for them and provide for them in ways they never anticipated. . . .*" [65: 2–3][250] And in this vein, Shaykh Abū al-ʿAbbās (al-Mursī)° said, as part of his formal personalized supplication: "And grant me this and that," adding, "and unalloyed provisions that engender neither veiling in this life nor reckoning, questioning, or punishment in the life to come, as we repose[251] on the carpet of knowledge of monotheism and the religious law, safe from undisciplined passion and cupidity."[252]

272. [253]Beware of planning in competition with God*. One who plans in competition with God is like a slave whose master sends him to a town to have a garment made. The slave enters this town and says, "Where shall I live, whom shall I marry?" He busies himself with these issues, directs his energy toward all of this, and abandons what his master has ordered him to do, until the latter summons him. His recompense will be that the master will sanction him by

248. According to *I.Q.*, 104 nt. 1, al-Suyūṭī cited a report via similar language in his *al-Darr al-manthūr*.

249. *I.Q.*, 104; *Shaqrūn*, 56; *J.K.*, 181: *bi riḍāh*; *J.K.*, 152: *bi al-muwāfaqah lah*.

250. *N.K.*, 181 cites the verse in full.

251. *Shaqrūn*, 56; *J.K.*, 152: *wa lā ʿiqāba fī al-ākhirah ʿalā bisāṭ ʿilm al-tawḥīd . . .* ; *I.Q.*, 104; *N.K.*, 182: *wa lā ʿiqāba fī al-ākhirah fa ahluhu ʿalā bisāṭ ʿilm al-tawḥīd. . . .*

252. *I.Q.*, 104; *al-ṭamʿ*; *Shaqrūn*, 56; *N.K.*, 182; *J.K.*, 152: *al-ṭabʿ*.

253. Here *J.K.*, 152 goes to what I have at ¶ 279, beginning with the Qurʾānic verse (of which *J.K.* gives only part) and continuing up to the end of ¶ 280 (*J.K.*, 153). *J.K.*, 154 then returns to what I have at ¶ 272.

cutting him off and refusing to allow him into his presence, because of his having allowed himself to be distracted by his own concerns away from the rights of his master. This is what you are like, O believer. God dispatched you to this abode and commanded you to serve Him, having taken it upon Himself to arrange things for you, out of his benevolence. But when your preoccupation with making arrangements for yourself distracts you from the rights of your Master, you veer from the path of guidance and enter upon the path of destruction.

273. The likeness of one who plans in competition with God and one who does not is that of two slaves who belong to a king. As for one of them, he busies himself with his master's affairs, paying little attention to his own food or clothing. Indeed, his ambition is merely to serve his master. And this distracts him from the fortunes of his self. As for the other slave, any time the master summons him, he finds him washing his own clothing, tending his own mount, and sprucing up his own appearance. The first slave is more likely than the second to gain his master's appreciation. Indeed, slaves are merely purchased for their masters, not for themselves. In a similar fashion, you only see the perceptive, fortunate servant busying himself with the rights of God and honoring His commands and prohibitions, at the expense of those things his self loves and values. As a result, God* comes to take care of all of his affairs and turns to him with plenteous bounty, because of his sincerity in trusting in God, in accordance with His statement, "*And whoever trusts in God, He will suffice them. . . .*" [65: 3][254] Heedless people are not like this. You only find them pursuing worldly interests and those things that enable them to fulfill their undisciplined passions.

254. *N.K.*, 184 cites the verse in full.

274. The likeness of humans in their relationship with God in this abode is that of a child with its mother. No mother would cease to arrange the affairs of a child in her custody, nor would she ever place that child outside the purview of her care.[255] Likewise is the believer with God, who takes it upon Himself to take good care of the believer, in the context of which He delivers bounties to him and protects him from tribulations.

275. The likeness of people in this world is that of a slave to whom a master says, "Go to such and such land. And manage your affairs so that you will be able to travel from it through the steppes of such and such. Take all of the equipment you need and make the necessary preparations." Now, if this master has granted this slave permission to do all of this, it goes without saying that he permits him to consume what he needs to sustain himself, in order to be able to pursue the procurement of this equipment and make these necessary preparations.

276. Similar is the likeness of people with God: He has brought them into being in this abode and commanded them to take from it the necessary provisions to make their return to Him. Thus, He* said, "*And gather the necessary provisions. And the best provision is God-consciousness. . . .*" [2: 197][256] It goes without saying that when He commands them to acquire the necessary provisions for the Afterlife He permits them to take from this world that which will assist them in acquiring what is necessary for them to make it to the Afterlife and to ready and prepare themselves for their return to Him.

255. *Shaqrūn*, 58: *lam takun al-umm li tada'a tadbīra waladihā fī kafālatihā wa lā tukhrijahu min ri'āyatihā*"; *I.Q.*, 106; *N.K.*, 184: *lam takun al-umm li tada'a tadbīra waladihā min kafālatihā*. Cf. *J.K.*, 156: *wa lam takun al-umm tamna'u waladahā min kafālatihā wa lā an taḥjubahu min ri'āyatihā*.

256. *N.K.*, 185 cites the verse in full.

277. The likeness of people in their relationship with God is that of a hireling whom a king brings to his home and commissions to do a job. This king would not bring this hireling to his home to employ him and then leave him with no food supplies. For, he is too noble for this. Likewise is the relationship between people and God. This world is God's "home," the hireling is you, the job is obedience, and the remuneration is Paradise. And God would not commission you for a job without delivering to you what you need to assist you therein.

278. The likeness of people with God* is that of a slave whom a king commands to occupy the land of such and such, fight the enemy there, and prosecute the jihad against them. It goes without saying that when he commands him to do this he gives him permission to take, in good faith, what he needs from the supplies stored in this land to assist him in fighting the enemy. Likewise are people: God* has commanded them to fight the self and Satan and to prosecute the jihad against them,[257] as in His statement, "*Wage jihad in the cause of God as it should be waged. He has selected you.*" [22: 78] And He said, "*Verily Satan is an enemy to you, so take him as an enemy.*" [35: 6] Now, when He commands people[258] to wage war against this enemy, He implicitly grants them permission to take from what His earth brings forth[259] whatever they need to assist them in waging war against Satan, since, were they to abandon food and drink they would not be able to obey or actively serve Him with any vigor.

279. The likeness of people with God is that of a king who has several slaves for whom he builds accommodations, which he

257. *I.Q.*, 107; *Shaqrūn*, 58; *N.K.*, 187: *amarahum al-ḥaqq subḥānahu wa taʿālā bi muḥārabat al-nafs wa al-shayṭān wa mujāhadatihimā*; *J.K.*, 157: *amarahum al-ḥaqq subḥānahu bi muḥārabat al-nafs wa al-shayṭān wa mujāhadat al-nufūs*.

258. *I.Q.*, 107; *Shaqrūn*, 58; *N.K.*, 187: *fa lammā amara al-ʿabd*; *J.K.*, 157: *fa kamā amara al-ʿabd*.

259. *I.Q.*, 107; *Shaqrūn*, 58; *N.K.*, 187: *min manābit arḍih*; *J.K.*, 157: *min minnatih*.

embellishes and beautifies. He plants its gardens and tops it off with a supply of delicious foods, all of this away from where the slaves are presently housed. His aim, however, is ultimately to transfer them to these new accommodations. Now, if he has this much concern for them, as reflected in what he has stored and prepared for them upon their relocation, do you think that he would prohibit them from partaking of his bounties and superabundance of food in their present location, having prepared for them this magnificent affair and enormous favor? This is the likeness of people with God. He placed them in this world and prepared Paradise for them. He does not want to deprive them of the things of this world but rather to enable them to sustain their existence.[260] [261]Thus, He* said, "*Take of the good things and work righteous deeds.*" [23: 51] And He said, "*O you who believe, take of the good things which We have provided you.*" [2: 172] Now, if He has stored away for you that which is everlasting and offered it to you as a favor, He would not deny you access to that which is fleeting. He simply denies you that part of the latter which He has not decreed for you. And what He has not decreed for you is not for you to have.

280. A person who is worried about his affairs in this world and is heedless regarding his preparations for his Afterlife is like a person who happens upon a predatory animal who intends to eat him. Then a fly lands on him, at which time he busies himself with repelling and fanning away the fly instead of avoiding the predatory animal. The truth is that this person is an idiot, devoid of reason. Had he any

260. *J.K.*, 158: *wa akl mā yuqīmu wujūdahum*; *I.Q.*, 108; *Shaqrūn*, 59: *N.K.*, 188: *wa lākin mā yuqīmu bihi wujūdahum. J.K.*, 158 stops and skips at this point to the middle of ¶ 280. See nt. 263, below.

261. *J.K.* begins this segment with the last sentence of *J.K.*, 152 and goes to the end of *J.K.*, 153, i.e., from "He*" of ¶ 279 to "idiocy" of ¶280.

sense, his concern about this lion and his pouncing on and attacking him would have distracted him from thinking about this fly. This is the likeness of those who concern themselves with the affairs of this world to the exclusion of preparing for the Afterlife. And this is an indication of their idiocy, [262]since, were they people of reason and understanding, they would prepare themselves for the Afterlife, about which they shall be questioned and in which they shall be brought front and center, and they would not busy themselves with the matter of worldly provisions. Indeed, being concerned about this compared to being concerned about the Afterlife is like being concerned about the fly compared to being concerned about being blindsided and attacked by the lion.

281. One who honors sacred trusts is like a king's slave who sees himself as having no right to his master's property. He neither consistently saves nor spends what is entrusted to him but limits himself to his master's preference.[263] When he understands that his master wants him to abstain from spending, he abstains, because his master wants him to, not because he wants to, until his master decides where to direct this money, at which time he spends it where he understands his master wants it spent. By abstaining in this way, this slave incurs no blame, for he abstains in the interest of his master, not in the interest of himself. This is the likeness of those who have supersensory knowledge of God. If they exert themselves, they do so in His interest; if they abstain, they do so for Him. They seek that in which His pleasure resides. And in their exertion and abstention they seek only Him.

262. *J.K.*, 158 resumes here.

263. *J.K.*, 158: *wa lā badhlihi illā mā ikhtārahu al-sayyidu lahu; Shaqrūn*, 60: *wa lā budda lahu minhu bal ʿalā mā yakhtāruhu al-sayyid; N.K.*, 190: *wa lā budda lahu minhu illā mā yakhtāruhu al-sayyid; I.Q.*, 109: *wa lā badala lahu wa lā yakhtāru illā mā yakhtāruhu al-sayyid lahu.*

282. These are faithful trustees, grand servants and noble devotees whom God has freed from enslavement to vain influences, as a result of which they neither incline toward the latter with love nor pursue them with affection. Rather, the love and affection for God that He has caused to settle in their hearts, along with His grandeur and majesty that fills their breasts, prevents them from this. Thus, they come to treat the things they possess as if these were still part of God's treasury prior to being transferred to them, based on their recognition that God* is the Owner of both them and that over which He has granted them ownership.

283. This is a clarification to those who ponder and a guide to those who seek insight: Whoever abandons planning for himself, God will take it upon Himself to plan for him in the best of ways! Planning for oneself, however, is of two types: 1) praiseworthy planning; and 2) condemnable planning.

284. Condemnable planning is every plan that revolves around one's self and its fortunes, with nothing in it for God, such as planning to engage in some act of disobedience or pleasure with reckless abandon,[264] or planning to engage in an act of worship in order to be seen among men and enhance one's reputation, and other such things. All of this is condemnable. For, it leads either to punishment or veiling.

285. One who knows the value of reason will be too ashamed before God* to use it to plan for things that do not bring him closer to God and are not a means of attaining His love. Indeed, reason is the best thing that God has granted His servants. For He* conferred the bounty of existence and continued sustenance upon everything He created. As such, all things share in these. And since all things share in this, God* wanted to distinguish humans among them. So

264. *J.K.*, 160; *Shaqrūn*, 61; *N.K.*, 192: *bi wujūd al-ghaflah*; *I.Q.*, 110: *bi wujūd 'aql.*

He gave humans reason and aided them through it and thereby placed them above the animals, thus completing His favor upon humanity. Indeed, through reason, its full capacity, radiance, and light, the interests of this world and the Next are realized. But using the bounty of reason merely to plan for the vanities of this world, which has no true value before God*, is a rejection of the bounty of reason.

286. It is sounder, more fitting, better, and more appropriate that this bounty be directed toward a concern with putting one's affair aright at the resurrection, showing gratitude to the One who conferred it and caused His light to flood down upon one. Thus, do not exhaust your reason, which God has granted you as a favor, on planning for the life of this world, which, as the Prophet* said, is "a putrid corpse." In fact, he said to the Companion al-Daḥḥāk: "What do you eat?" "Meat and yogurt," he replied. "Then where do these go?" he asked. "To where you well know, O Messenger of God." The Prophet then said, "Verily, God has made that which comes out of humans a similitude for the life of this world."[265]

287. Praiseworthy planning, on the other hand, is planning for that which moves one closer to God*, such as planning in order to retire one's obligations regarding people's rights over one, either in terms of fulfilling your obligations to them or in terms of determining what may be rightfully exacted from them, or planning to make good on one's repentance to the Lord of all being and becoming, or thinking about ways to suppress destructive passions and the Deceptive Devil. All of this is praiseworthy, without doubt. And for this reason, the Prophet* said, "Pondering for an hour is better than seventy years of worship."[266]

265. The editors of *I.Q.* note that a hadith with almost identical wording appears in the *Musnad al-imām aḥmad*.

266. According to editors of *I.Q.*, 112, nt. 1, al-Suyūṭī cited this hadith in *al-Jāmiʿ al-ṣaghīr* (with sixty instead of seventy years) and indicated that it was weak. Ibn al-Jawzī also cited

288. Now, planning for the life of this world is of two types: 1) planning the affairs of this world for this world; and 2) planning the affairs of this world for the Afterlife.

289. Planning the affairs of this world for this world is to devise the means of amassing its delights, for the purpose of showing off and augmenting one's share thereof. And every time something is added to this, it increases one in heedlessness and self-deception. The telltale sign of this is that it takes one away from conformity to God's command and leads one to violations.

290. Planning the affairs of this life for the Afterlife, on the other hand, is like one who arranges his business[267] in order to profit lawfully therefrom, or to use it to bestow gratuitous favors upon the poor, or to protect his honor from people in general. Its telltale sign is the lack of amassing and storing up wealth but, rather, using it to rescue others from ruin, giving preference to them over other ways of spending it.

291. From this it becomes clear that not every one who seeks the benefits of this world is to be condemned. Rather, the condemned are those who seek these benefits for their selves, not for their Lord, for this world, not for the Afterlife. People fall, thus, into two categories: 1) those who seek the benefits of this world for this world; and 2) those who seek the benefits of this world for the Afterlife.

292. I heard our Shaykh Abū al-'Abbās al-Mursī° say: "One who has supersensory knowledge of God has no worldly nor otherworldly life; for the life of this world is for his Afterlife, and his Afterlife is for his Lord."

---

it in his book on fabricated hadiths. Al-Daylimī, meanwhile, cites it in his book *al-Firdaws*, with eighty instead of seventy years. In *Sunan abī dā'ūd*, 2: 407, however, part of the hadith in which the Prophet states that scholars are the heirs of the prophets also states that "the superiority of the learned over the simply worshipful is as that of a full-moon at night over the rest of the stars."

267. *I.Q.*, 112; *Shaqrūn*, 62; *N.K.*, 195: *yudabbir al-matājir*; *J.K.*, 163: *yurīd al-mutājarah*.

293. This is the light in which we should understand the ways of the Companions and Pious Ancestors, may God be pleased with them all. Every worldly enterprise they entered was for the purpose of drawing near to God and allying themselves with His pleasure. They were not simply seeking the life of this world, its embellishments and carnal pleasures. And for this reason, God* described them as He did in His statement, "*Muhammad is the Messenger of God, and those who are with him are severe on the non-believers but merciful among themselves. You see them bowing and prostrating, seeking favor from God along with His pleasure. . . .*" [48: 29][268] Now, what do you think of a people whom God loves and chose to accompany the Messenger of God* and to be directly addressed by His revelation?

294. Indeed, there is not a single believer, till the Day of Judgment, who does not owe the Companions an immeasurable debt of gratitude and who has not been aided by them in unforgettable ways. For, they are the ones who transmitted to us from the Prophet* wisdom and rules of life. And they clarified the permissible and the impermissible and explained of this what was general and what was specific in scope. They conquered whole regions and countries and subdued the people of polytheism and obstinacy. Indeed, the Prophet's*[269] statement accurately portrays them: "My Companions are like stars; through whichever of them you seek guidance you will be guided."[270]

295. Indeed, God* described them in the aforementioned noble verse with several attributes up to the point that He referred to

268. *N.K.*, 196 cites the verse in full.

269. *N.K.*, 197 adds *ṣalātan wa salāman dā'iman abadan* (consistent, eternal prayers and salutations).

270. The editors of *I.Q.*, 114, nt.1, note that Ibn Ḥazm cites this hadith in his *al-Iḥkām fī uṣūl al-aḥkām*, and remarks that Salām b. Sulaymān, who was in this chain, was known for relating fabricated hadith and that "this is surely one of them."

them as "*. . . seeking favor from God along with His pleasure. . . .*" [48: 29][271] This part of His* statement indicates that they only sought through what they were able to achieve in this world God's pleasure and bounteous favor. Thus, God says in another verse, "*In houses that God has permitted to be built and that His name be mentioned therein, in which men who neither business nor barter distract from the remembrance of God praise Him in the early morning and late afternoon.*" [24: 36–37] Now, He did not negate their involvement with the means of sustaining themselves, nor with commerce, selling, or buying. Thus, their wealth did not disqualify them from being praised, inasmuch as they recognized the rights of their Master regarding their wealth.

296. 'Abd Allāh b. 'Utbah said: On the day he was killed 'Uthmān b. 'Affān° had the equivalent of one hundred thousand, five hundred gold *dīnārs*, along with a million silver *dirhams* in holding with his treasurer.[272] He left a thousand horses and a thousand slaves, as well as real estate, including wells at Arīs, Khaybar, and Wādī al-Qurā, its total value amounting to two hundred thousand gold *dīnārs*. 'Amr b. al-'Āṣ left three hundred thousand[273] gold *dīnārs*. Al-Zubayr b. al-'Awāmm's wealth reached fifty thousand gold *dīnārs*, and he left behind a thousand horses and a thousand slaves. And 'Abd al-Raḥmān b. 'Awf's° wealth was too well known to mention.

297. But these worldly possessions occupied their hands, not their hearts. Whenever they lost any of it, they bore this patiently. And whenever they gained anything, they thanked God. God simply tested them with poverty in the beginning, to the point that their

271. *N.K.*, 198 cites the verse in full. Interestingly, *I.Q.* gives 59: 8 as the reference here.

272. *I.Q.*, 114; *Shaqrūn*, 64: *N.K.*, 199: *'inda khāzinihi yawma qutila*; *J.K.*, 167: *yawma qutila*.

273. *I.Q.*, 114; *Shaqrūn*, 64; *N.K.*, 199: *thalāthami'at alf dīnār*; *J.K.*, 167: *thamānimi'at alf dīnār*.

inner light was perfected and their inner conscience purified, at which time He disbursed this wealth to them. For, had they been given this before then, it might have diminished[274] them. But since it was given to them after they had been strengthened and grounded in certainty, they used it like a faithful trustee and fulfilled with it the dictates of the command of the Lord of all being and becoming: "*Spend of what He has bequeathed to you.* [57: 7]

298. Thus, again, worldly possessions occupied the hands of the Companions, not their hearts. And it should suffice as proof of this 'Umar b. al-Khaṭṭāb's° donating half of his wealth, Abū Bakr al-Ṣiddīq's° donating his entire wealth, 'Abd al-Raḥmān b. 'Awf's° donating seventy loaded camels, 'Uthmān b. 'Affān's° outfitting an entire army during the time of difficulty (at Tābūk), and other such examples of their generous deeds and noble constitution, may God be forever and ever pleased with them all. Thus the aforementioned verse included a declaration of both their outward and their inward integrity[275] and an affirmation of their praiseworthy attributes and glorious traits.

299. It becomes clear from all of this that planning is of two types: 1) planning the affairs of this world for this world, as is the habit of heedless, ignoble people of disconnectedness; and 2) planning the affairs of this world for the Afterlife, as was the way of the noble Companions and the Pious Ancestors, may God* be pleased with them all and make us among those who follow their example. Amen, nay, a million amens![276]

274. *I.Q.*, 115, nt. 1, indicates that the manuscript has *tu'khadh minhum* ("it might have been taken from them"). They posit, however, "*ta'khudh*," in agreement with *Shaqrūn*, 64, *N.K.*, 200, and *J.K.*, 167.

275. *I.Q.*, 116; *Shaqrūn*, 65; *N.K.*, 202: *tazkīyah*; *J.K.*, 168: *tadhkīyah*.

276. *I.Q.*, 116: *Shaqrūn*, 65; *N.K.*, 202: *bal alf alf āmīn*; *J.K.*, 168 omits this.

SECTION

God's Private Address to His Servant[277]

300. We shall mention[278] in this section a private address from God* to His servant, spoken through the invisible caller from the depths of true realities, regarding the matter of planning and procuring provisions.

301. O servant, lend Me your ears as you bear witness, and you will receive more from Me.[279] Listen intently, for I am not far from you. ∞[280]You existed through My planning for you before you existed for your self. So be for your self by not being for it. I took care of your self before you appeared on the scene. And I continue to take care of it now.

302. ∞I am alone in creating and fashioning. And I am alone in ruling and planning. You did not share in My creating or fashioning.

277. This heading is my addition, which I add to parallel the heading given at the beginning of the next section. *I.Q.*, *Shaqrūn*, and *J.K.*, simply begin this section with "*faṣl.*" (Section). *N.K.*, 203, however, gives *faṣl* then adds between square brackets *munājāt al-ḥaqq ta'ālā* (A Private Address from God The Exalted).

278. *I.Q.*, 117; *Shaqrūn*, 65; *N.K.*, 203: *faṣlun nadhkuru fīh*; *J.K.*, 169 has no mention of "*nadhkuru fīh*.

279. *I.Q.*, 117; *Shaqrūn*, 65: *N.K.*, 203: *ya'tika minnī*; *J.K.*, 169: *ya'tika min Allāh*.

280. In addition to where already indicated in the translation, *J.K.*, inserts *ayyuhā al-'abd* (O servant) at the beginning of every new paragraph, according to his parsing of the text, in contradistinction to both *I.Q.* and *Shaqrūn*. I have indicated where *J.K.* inserts this formula with the symbol "∞".

So do not try to share in My ruling and planning. ∞I am The Planner for My kingdom, and I have no helper in this regard. I am alone in My rule. Thus I have no need for a vizier.

303. O My servant, do not place your wants on the same level as those of the One who planned for you before you came to exist. And do not confront with obstinacy the One who accustomed you to being looked upon with favor. ∞I accustomed you to being looked upon with favor. So accustom Me to your giving up planning for yourself in competition with Mine.

304. Do you plan in competition with Me out of doubt,[281] after all of this experience; out of confusion, after all of this clarification; because you are lost, after the clarity of all of this guidance? You have already surrendered to me the administration of My kingdom—and you are part of My kingdom. So do not challenge My Lordship. And do not oppose Me by planning for yourself in the face of My divinity.

305. ∞When have I ever cast you into reliance solely upon yourself, such that you should have to consign yourself to yourself?[282] And when have I delegated anything in My kingdom to anyone other than Me, such that I would delegate any of this to you? When has anyone for whom I planned ever been disappointed? And when has anyone whom I aided ever been forsaken?

306. O servant, let your preoccupation with serving Me direct you away from pursuing disbursements from Me. And let your positive expectations of Me prevent you from impugning My Lordship. One who is beneficent should never be suspected of ill; and one who is mighty should never be challenged. One who is

281. *I.Q.*, 118; *Shaqrūn*, 66; *N.K.*, 204: *a shakkan … ḥīratan … ḍalālan*; *J.K.*, 170: *a shākkun … ḥīratun … ḍalālun.*

282. *I.Q.*, 118: *Shaqrūn*, 66; *N.K.*, 204: *taḥtāl ʿalayka*; *J.K.*, 170: *taḥtāl ʿalayya.*

indomitable should never be opposed; and one who is wise should never be objected to. Nor should one ever fret in the care of one who is gracious.

307. ∞One who forsakes his will in deference to Me shall attain success. And one who relies on Me shall be shown the way to easing his affairs. A servant who does not move except in My behalf shall earn entitlement to My assistance. And one who holds on to his relationship with Me holds on to the strongest of bonds.

308. O servant, We want you to want Us and no one along with Us. We want you to choose Us and no one along with Us. It pleases Us that We should suffice you and that no one other than Us suffices you. Just as you have surrendered to Me planning the affairs of My earth and My heavens and the monopoly over handing down rulings and judgments therein, surrender to Me existing for My sake. After all, you belong Me. And do not plan alongside My planning; for you are already with Me in my plans. Take Me as your agent, and trust in Me as your guarantor. I will remunerate you bounteously and grant you exalted honor.

309. ∞Woe unto you! We have exalted you in stature beyond having to tend to your own affairs. So do not debase yourself! O you whom We have raised in stature, do not be debased by consigning yourself to other than Us. ∞O you whom we have honored, woe unto you! You are too exalted in Our sight for Us to preoccupy you with anything other than Us.

310. To be in My presence is the reason I created and addressed you. And it is through the attractive power of My providence that I draw you thereto. If you preoccupy yourself with your self, I will veil you. And if you follow your self's undisciplined passions, I will cast you out. But if you transcend these, I will draw you near to Me. And if you ingratiate yourself with Me by turning away from other than Me, I will love you.

311. O servant, no one who challenges Me believes in Me. And no who plans despite My planning for him restricts divinity to Me. No one who complains to other than Me of what I visit upon them is pleased with Me. And no one who chooses anyone alongside Me chooses Me. No one who does not surrender to My might conforms to My command.

312. ∞Were you to seek a way to plan for your self, this would constitute an act of ignorance on your part. How much more would this be the case were you actually to plan? Were you to choose anyone else alongside Me, this would not be fair. How much more would this be the case were you actually to choose someone over Me?

313. O servant, it is enough ignorance on your part that you settle for what you have but not with what I have. I choose for you that you choose Me. Shall you then choose someone over Me?[283]

314. ∞O you who are worried about his self. Were you to consign it to Us, you would find rest. Woe unto you! Only divine lordship can carry the burdens of planning. Frail humanity is not strong enough to carry these. ∞Woe unto you! You are carried, so do not try to be a carrier. We want to relieve you. So don't burden your self.

315. O servant, I have commanded you to serve Me, while I guaranteed your share of disbursements from Me.[284]You have neglected My command[285] and doubted My guarantee, while I had not simply restricted Myself to guaranteeing; I actually disbursed! Nor did I restrict myself to simple disbursement; I disbursed exemplarily. And I directed an address in this regard to those of understanding: "*And in the heavens are your provisions and what you are promised. By the Lord of the heavens and the earth, it is indeed a truth*

283. *I.Q.*, 120; *Shaqrūn*, 67: *a fa takhtāru ʿalayya*; *J.K.*, 173: *fa takhtāru ʿalayya*; *N.K.*, 206: *fa kayfa yalīqu bika an takhtāra ʿalayya.*

284. *N.K.*, 207 adds here *wa akhbaʾtu lak jannatī.*

285. *N.K.*, 207 adds here *wa ṭaʿimta fīmā iddakharta.*

as plain as the fact that you speak." [51: 22–23] I have provided for those who are heedless of Me and who disobey Me. How could I not provide for those who obey and call upon Me?

316. ∞Woe unto you! One who plants a tree will surely water it. And the one who supplies creation is the one who fashioned it. From Me came the act of bringing things into existence. And upon Me is the perpetuation of their supplies. From Me came the act of creating. And upon Me is the perpetuation of provisions. Shall I admit you to My abode but then deny you My hospitality? Shall I bring you forth into My creation but then deny you My assistance? ∞ Shall I bring you into existence but then deny you My goodness? For you I made available My kindness. And in you I manifested My mercy. And because I was not satisfied with the life of this world for you,[286] I stored away for you My Paradise. And I was not even satisfied with this for you: I went on to gift you the benefit of seeing Me!

317. Now, if these are My actions, how can you doubt My favoring you? Choose Me.[287] And do not choose anyone over Me. And turn your heart in sincerity toward Me. If you do this, I will show you the marvels of My kindness and the wonders of My goodness. And I will gratify your inner conscience with witnessing Me.

318. ∞I have made manifest the path of the People of Realization and clear the hallmarks of guidance to those who have been granted success.[288] Thus, based on their recognition of what is right, those of certainty[289] surrender to Me. And, based on clear evidence,

286. I.Q., 121: *wa mā qana'tu laka bi al-dunyā*; *Shaqrūn*, 68: *J.K.*, 173; *N.K.*, 208: *wa mā qana'tu bi al-dunyā.*

287. I.Q., 122; *Shaqrūn*, 68; N.K., 208: *fa'khtarnī*; *J.K.*, 173: *takhayyarnī.*

288. I.Q., 122; N.K., 208; *la qad aẓhartu al-ṭarīq li ahl al-taḥqīq wa bayyantu ma'ālim al-hudā li dhawī al-tawfīq*; *Shaqrūn*, 68; N.K., 208: *la qad ẓaharat al-ṭarīq li ahl al-taḥqīq wa bayyantu ma'ālim al-hudā li dhawī al-tawfīq*; *J.K.*, 174: *la qad ẓaharat al-ṭarīq li ahl al-taḥqīq wa tabayyanat ma'ālim al-hudā li dhawī al-tawfīq.*

289. I.Q., 122; *Shaqrūn*, 68; N.K., 208: *al-mūqinūn*; *J.K.*, 174: *al-muwaffaqīn.*

the believers[290] place their trust in Me. They know that I am better for them than they are for themselves and that My planning for them is more fitting than their planning for themselves. Thus, they yield in surrender to My Lordship and cast themselves before Me, entrusting their affair to Me. I thus remunerate them for this with contentment in their souls, light in their minds, supersensory knowledge in their hearts, and a realization of My closeness in their inner being. This is in this life. Then, when they come before Me (after the resurrection) I have in store for them that I will exalt their station and elevate their place. And when I admit them to My other-worldly abode, they shall have[291] what no eye has seen, no ear has heard and the heart of no human has ever had occur to it.

319. O servant, I have not demanded uninterrupted service from you during the time you have ahead of you. So do not demand of Me uninterrupted allocations during this time. But whenever I place a duty upon you, I take it upon Myself to support you therein. And when I ask you to serve Me, I provide for your sustenance.

320. Know that I do not forget you, even if you forget Me. Indeed, I thought of you before you ever thought of Me. My providing for you is never-ending, even if you disobey Me. Now, if I am this way despite your turning away from Me, how do you think I will be if you devote yourself to Me. ∞You have not properly assessed my power, if you do not surrender to My might. And you do not acknowledge the reality of My goodness, if you do not comply with My command. But don't turn away from Me; for you will not find anyone whom you can substitute for Me. And do not be deceived by others besides Me; for no one will relieve you of your need for Me.

290. *I.Q.*, 122; *Shaqrūn*, 69; *N.K.*, 208: *al-mu'minūn*; *J.K.*, 174: *al-mutawakkilūn*.

291. *I.Q.*, 122; *Shaqrūn*, 69; *N.K.*, 209: *wa lahum idhā adkhaltuhum*; *J.K.*, 174: *wa lahum 'alayya idhā adkhaltuhum*.

321. ∞I am your creator, by My power. And I am the extender of My kindness to you. And just as there is no creator other than Me, there is no provider other than Me. ∞Shall I create creatures and then consign them to other than Me,[292] while I am The Gracious One? Shall I deny people My goodness, while I am The Granter of Bounty?

322. Trust in Me, O servant, for I am the Lord of servants. Step out of your wants over to Me; I will take you to exactly what you want. Remember My past acts of graciousness. And do not forget the duty of requiting love.

His Private Supplication, May God Be Pleased with Him[293]

323. My God, I am the poor one, even in the midst of my wealth. How could I not be poor, then, in the midst of my poverty? I am the ignorant one, even in my state of knowledge. How could I not be ignorant in my state of ignorance?

324. My God, from me come things that are commensurate with my depravity. From You come things that are commensurate with Your grace. ^If good things come from me, they come by Your favor, for which I owe You a debt of gratitude. If bad things come from me, they come by Your justice, by which You sustain Your case against me.

325. My God, how could You entrust my affair to anyone else, while You have taken it upon Yourself to act in my behalf?[294] And

292. *N.K.*, 210 continues to the end of this section with *fa annā al-mutafaḍḍil ʿalā al-ʿibād bi birrī wa karamī wa khayrī*. He omits, however, what *I.Q.* has up to the end of this segment.

293. In this section, in addition to where it is indicated in the translation, *J.K.* inserts *ilāhī* (My God) at the beginning of every paragraph according to his parsing of the text, in contradistinction to *I.Q.*, *Shaqrūn*, and *N.K.* I have indicated this with the symbol "^".

294. *I.Q.*, 124; *Shaqrūn*, 71: *kayfa takilunī wa qad tawakkalta lī*; *N.K.*, 211: *kayfa tukilunī ilā nafsī wa qad tawakkalta lī*; *J.K.*, 176: *kayfa takilunī ilā nafsī wa qad tawakkaltu ʿalayk*.

how could I be harmed, while You are my aid to victory? Or how could I be disappointed, while I am well received by You?

326. Here am I seeking to ingratiate myself with You by means of my poverty. But how can I ingratiate myself through that which cannot possibly reach You? Or how can I complain to You of my condition, while its reality never escapes You? Or how can I translate to you the contents of my mind, while they emerge from and to You? Or how can my hopes be dashed, while they have made their way to You?[295] Or how can my circumstances not be good, while You are their sustainer and *terminus ad quem*?

327. My God, how kind You are to me, despite my ignorance.[296] And how merciful You are to me, despite my vile acts. How close You are to me, and how far I am from You. But how gracious You are to me. So what is it that veils me from You?

328. My God, just as my depravity renders me dumb, Your generosity enables me to speak. And every time my character traits cause me to lose hope, Your benevolence restores my aspirations.

329. My God, one whose good qualities are bad, how can their bad qualities not be bad? And one whose true state of affairs is nothing but empty pretense, how can their empty pretenses be anything but empty pretenses?

330. [297]^My God, how can I have any resolve, while Your might is overpowering? And yet how can I not have any resolve, while You are the issuer of commands?[298]

331. ^My fluctuating about in worldly impressions makes great the distance between me and my desired destination. So set me on a path of service to You that will deliver me to You.

295. Here *J.K.*,177 jumps to ¶ 330.
296. *N.K.*, 212: *ma'a aẓīm jahlī.*
297. *J.K.*, 177 resumes here.
298. *I.Q.*, 125: *Shaqrūn*, 71–72; *N.K.*, 212: *kayfa a'zim wa anta al-qāhir wa kayfa lā a'zim wa anta al-āmir*; *J.K.*, 177: *kayfa uhzam wa anta al-qāhir wa kayfa lā u'azz wa anta al-āmir.*

332. ^How can Your existence be proved through that whose existence is contingent upon You? Can something other than You be more manifest than You, such that it could make You manifest? ^Since when were You absent, such that You would require proof of Your presence? ^And since when did You become so distant that worldly impressions would become that which delivers unto You?

333. My God, the eye that does not see You watching over it is blind. And any deal in which one does not seek Your love as a part of their profit will result in loss.

334. My God, my humiliation is clear before You. And my condition is not lost on You. From You I ask to be delivered to You. And through You I prove Your existence. So guide me, by Your light, to You. And stand me, by the sincerity of my servanthood, before You.

335. My God, teach me from Your undisclosed knowledge. And protect me through the secret of Your protected name. Grant me the realizations of the people of closeness to You. And take me along the path of the people who are attracted to You. Relieve me, through Your planning for me, of the need to plan for myself, and through Your choosing for me of the need to choose for myself. Show me the sources of my compulsions. Free me from the humiliations of my self. And cleanse me of all my doubts and associationism (*shirk*), before I settle in my grave.

336. In You I seek aid to victory; so aid me. Upon You I rely; so do not consign me to any other. To You I direct my requests; so do not deny me. And Your favor I hope to attain; so do not disappoint me. With Your honor I associate myself; so do not banish me. And at Your door I beckon; so do not turn me away.

337. My God, Your planning and execution have overcome me. And my undisciplined passion for those strong carnal pleasures has imprisoned me. So be my aid to the point of granting me victory and

insight.[299] And enrich me, through Your bounteousness, such that by Your bounteousness I may be freed of the need to ask.

338. You are the one whose light radiates in the hearts of Your saints. And You are the one who dispels all others from the inner consciousness of Your loved ones. You are their comforter when the universe fills them with alienation. And You are the one who guides them such that they are able to discern the guideposts.

339. ^What has one who fails to find You found? And what is it that one who finds You loses? Whoever is pleased with a would-be substitute for You will be frustrated. And whoever desires an alternative to You will lose. How can anyone place their hope in other than You, while You have never withheld Your goodness? And how can anyone direct their requests to other than You, while You have never altered Your habit of graciousness?

340. ^O He who has caused His loved ones to taste the sweetness of His intimacy, as a result of which they stand before Him in flattery; O He who has clothed His saints in the garb of His awe, as a result of which they stand seeking to draw glory from His glory: You are the Rememberer before those who give remembrance. And You are the initiater of goodness before worshippers turn to you for it. You are the one who gives generously, by giving before requesters request. Indeed, You are the one who donates to us and then borrows from us of what You have donated. Call on me, by Your mercy, that I may make my way to You. And pull me, by your benevolence, that I may commit myself to You.

341. My God, my hope in You never dissipates, even as I disobey You, just as my fear of You never leaves me,[300] even as I obey You.

299. *I.Q.*, 126; *Shaqrūn*, 73; *J.K.*, 178: *ḥattā tanṣuranī wa tubaṣṣiranī*; *N.K.*, 214: *ḥattā tanṣuranī wa tanṣura bī*.

300. *I.Q.*, 127; *Shaqrūn*, 74; *N.K.*, 215: *khawfī lā yuzāyilunī*; *J.K.*, 179: *khawfī lā yazāl yuzāyidunī*.

The universe has pushed me toward You. And my knowledge of your generosity has brought me to You. How can I be disappointed, while You are my hope? Or how can I be humiliated, while You are the one upon whom I rely? How can I seek glory, while You have grounded me in humility? Or how can I not seek glory, while You have linked me with You? How could I not be poor, while You have placed me in poverty? Or how can I be poor, while you have enriched me through Your generosity?

342. You are the One besides whom there is no god. You have disclosed Yourself to everything; so nothing is ignorant of You. And You have disclosed Yourself to me in everything; so I see You manifested in everything. You are, thus, The Manifest to everything!

343. O He who settled on the Throne through His mercifulness, such that the Throne disappeared into His mercifulness, as the universe disappeared into His Throne, You have crushed worldly impressions with divine impressions. And You have obliterated all others through the oceans of constellations of light.

344. ^O He who is veiled behind the canopies of His might such that eyes cannot see Him. O He who appears through the perfection of His brilliance such that inner consciences realize His grandeur. How can You be hidden, while You are The Manifest? Or how can You disappear, while You are The Ever-Present Overseer?[301]

345. God, send Your blessings and salutations upon our master Muhammad, the unlettered prophet, the pure, the blameless, and upon his family, blessings that undo knots, ease tribulations, terminate harm, and make difficult matters simple, blessings that please

301. *I.Q.*, 128 and *Shaqrūn*, 75 agree on this ending. *J.K.*, 180 ends with *wa Allāhu a'lam wa ṣalla Allāhu 'alā sayyidinā muḥammad wa 'alā ālihi wa sallama. N.K.*, 216 ends with *wa Allāh al-muwaffiq wa bihi asta'īn wa ṣalla Allāh 'alā sayyidinā muḥammad wa 'alā ālihi wa ṣaḥbihi ajma'īn.*

You and please him and through which You come to be pleased with us, O Lord of all being and becoming.

With this, by God's assistance, the book, *The Bride-Groom's Crown Containing Instructions on Refining the Self*, by Ibn 'Aṭā' Allāh al-Sakandarī, is brought to completion.[302]

302. This closing appears only in *Shaqrūn*, 75.

INDEX

INDEX